The Growth of the Person:

Psychology on Trial

PSYCHOLOGY ON TRIAL

The Growth of the Person

GRACE M.H. GAYLE, PhD

Essence PUBLISHING

Belleville, Ontario, Canada

THE GROWTH OF THE PERSON:
PSYCHOLOGY ON TRIAL

Copyright © 2001, Grace M.H. Gayle, Ph.D.

All Rights Reserved. No part of this publication may be reproduced, stored in a retrieval system or transmitted in any form or by any means – electronic, mechanical, photocopy, recording or any other – except for brief quotations in printed reviews, without the prior permission of the author.

All Scripture quotations, unless otherwise specified, are from *The Holy Bible, King James Version*. Copyright © 1977, 1984, Thomas Nelson Inc., Publishers.

Scripture quotations marked NKJV are taken from the New King James Version. Copyright © 1979, 1980, 1982. Thomas Nelson Inc., Publishers.

ISBN: 1-55306-227-2

Cover photo by Dr. Brenda Gayle-Anyiwe

Essence Publishing is a Christian Book Publisher dedicated to furthering the work of Christ through the written word.
For more information, contact:
44 Moira Street West, Belleville, Ontario, Canada K8P 1S3.
Phone: 1-800-238-6376. Fax: (613) 962-3055.
E-mail: info@essencegroup.com
Internet: www.essencegroup.com

Printed in Canada
by
Essence PUBLISHING

The Christian ideal has not been tried and found wanting. It has been found difficult; and left untried.

G.K. Chesterton
What's Wrong with the World

Mr. and Mrs. R.V.H. Gayle Sr.

In gratitude to God for His divine grace.

*To the Lord Jesus Christ whose shed blood bought me life.
To Him be honour and glory and praise forever.*

To the Holy Spirit who enabled me to write this work.

*In loving memory of a wonderful father,
Rudolph Vernon Hope Gayle,
whom God used to show me His magnificent light,*

and

*dedicated to my beloved mother,
Brenda Carmen Gayle,
who has always been my earthly angel.*

*To all my family members and friends who gave me their
prayers and support.*

Psychology is the eggshell. When it has been cracked and removed the egg is still there—white, yolk and embryo. Like any shell, it often has its bubbles.

Grace Gayle

TABLE OF CONTENTS

Figures 11
Preface 13

I. CLEARING THE UNDERGROWTH
    1. Controversial Issues 21

II. THE STRUCTURE OF THE PERSON
    2. Choosing a Model - Discussion 65
    3. The Healthy Person:
       mens sana in corpore sano? 85
    4. The Special People 97
    5. A Model of Man 103

III. THE DEVELOPING PERSON
    6. A Model of the Development of the Person 119

IV. DISPARITIES
    7. Introduction 155

8. "Ye Must Be Born Again"....................159
9. Self-control versus Holiness..................163
10. The Real Living Being......................167
11. Assurance versus Open-mindedness
    and Closed-mindedness......................175
12. Self-concept versus Spirit....................183
13. "Congruence" versus Godliness...............191
14. Faulty Extremes versus Temperance
    and God-control...........................197
15. Human "Morality" versus Divine Love.........205
16. Divine Love 215
17. Discipline................................221
18. Trust in God versus Basic Anxiety.............229

Conclusion: Sabbatismos........................239
Endnotes 245

Figures

Fig. 1 - The Nature of Man. 45
Fig. 2 - Christian Model: The Nature of Man 57
Fig. 3 - Model of Man 106
Fig. 4 - Development of the Person 131
Fig. 5 - The Constitution of Regenerate Man:
       Relevance of Psychological Constructs
       to Biblical Experience 136
Fig. 6 - Aspects of Development and Relationship
       in Discipleship 225
Fig. 7 - Trust in God versus Basic Anxiety 234

Preface

And he is the head of the body, the church: who is the beginning, the firstborn from the dead; that in all things he might have the preeminence.
                                                                Colossians 1:18

It is reasonable to take the view that in order to find the true meaning of the term "Christian," we must refer to the dogma of the pristine Church of the first century AD. Today, in the twenty-first century, the numberless definitions and interpretations of the erstwhile revolutionary term "Christian" is bewildering. The history of the world seems to illustrate what now appears to be a rule that the advent of any revolutionary idea or experience is immediately assailed by dubious detractors, contenders and, more seriously, half-hearted adherents. The twentieth century has therefore tried to make sense of unparalleled contradictions in the use of the appellation "Christian." We are faced, among so many other absurdities, with the incongruity embedded in the now-popular term "Christian humanism" and we must somehow deal with a diversity of types in the world's population who attest to racist tendencies, partisan hatred and a fundamental belief in self-sufficiency, yet who claim to be Christian and who vie for exclusive rights in the use of this term.

The history of Christianity indicates that the disciples were first called Christians at Antioch on the Orontes. The Latin form, *Christian(o)i*, was first given as a nickname by Herod Agrippa II and Nero, among others, to those who called their distinctive faith "The Way." The Latin name meant "soldiers of Christ" or the "household of Christ" and was gladly accepted by those in Jerusalem and in outlying regions as far as Asia Minor who believed that Jesus of Nazareth was the Christ, the Messiah, very man yet very God. By AD 60 the term Christian was well established. This heterogeneous early Church, comprised of Jewish and Gentile converts, acknowledged that they were *"one body in Christ"* (Romans 12:5) and that they had been purchased with His own blood (Acts 20:28).

Obviously, the true meaning of Christianity is not to be found in the intellectual tenets which support the label *per se* but in what is actually enshrined in the heart of the individual, colouring his entire being and behaviour. It is therefore worthwhile to assert the experience of the heart in examining the depth of Christian doctrine. For the Christian following the pattern of the early Church, the desired goal, the chosen pathway, is the putting away or death of the old man—the corrupt nature—and the birth and growth of the new man involving the self submitted to the Lord Jesus Christ. In following the One who said, *"I am the way, the truth and the life"* (John 14:6), the individual expects that the excellence of His purity demands a high way (Isaiah 55:9) that is "strait" and "narrow" (Matthew 7:13,14). Nor was the early Church content, as some modernists are, with self-effort. They quickly recognized that this would only have served to cast them back into the throes of legalism and "self-assertism." What the early Church desired was the indwelling, controlling presence of the Lord Jesus Christ Himself. They were content with nothing less than the fulfillment of His promise: *"If a man love me, he will keep my words: and my Father will love him, and we will come unto him, and make our abode with him"* (John 14:23).

It is in this context and in this experience that the author attempts to present a Christian perspective of psychological teaching. The most compelling premise underlying every argument or disposition in this work is not a psychological but a theological one and takes the form of the uncompromising acceptance of Jesus Christ as the express image of the Person of God (Hebrews 1:3).

Given this fact, the human being must *"grow in grace, and in the knowledge of our Lord and Saviour Jesus Christ"* (2 Peter 3:18) in order to develop fully and perfectly as a person.

Psychology has been dedicated over the years to the study of the human mind (psyche) and human behaviour. This work insists that the study of psychology be carried out within the framework of, and with deference to, Christianity as enunciated by the experience of the early Church. This is to some extent a novel approach. It is time for us to join one of the greatest truces of the twentieth century, if only long enough to see where the real differences and similarities between Christianity and psychology lie. If the psychological term *mind* is to be whittled down to the purely intellectual, devoid of the affective and of the behavioural, then obviously the term would fall very far short of the description of the total person, an untenable position in light of psychology's alleged aims. If, as we know, however, the word *mind* in psychology is often geared to subsume the behavioural, the subjective and often the emotional as well as the intellectual, we see that the Christian perspective presents a no less comprehensive view. In fact, Christian theology lifts the concept of mind to the highest possible level of completion where true personhood is found.

> *Let this mind be in you, which was also in Christ Jesus: Who, being in the form of God, thought it not robbery to be equal with God: But made himself of no reputation, and took upon him the form of a servant, and... humbled himself, and became obedient unto death...* (Philippians 2:5-8).

Here we see the progression from internal life to behaviour or external expression of this life, and, in proper sequence, from vertical relationship with God to social commitment. It is evident from the preceding that the biblical understanding of *mind* has at least two meanings which supercede the intent and conviction of most modern psychological discussions. First, man's mind, in its broadest sense, may be transformed by the indwelling presence of God Himself. Second, this relationship with God can never be secondary nor subordinate to the horizontal social relationship.

Existentially, the religious and the psychological cannot be strangers. If we are to have an intellectual understanding of the breadth of their respective contributions to the growing person, we must more adequately appreciate the effect of each on the other. Although this work will not pretend to undertake this monumental task in all its aspects (for example, no mention is made of the effects of unethical educational and clinical practices sometimes found in schools, psychological or psychiatric clinics, on the spiritual life of the growing person), its objective continues to be the reconciliation, in as critical and uncompromising a manner as possible, of major psychological theory and finding, with basic Christian belief.

We are slowly beginning to see that, in the enterprise of understanding and facilitating the development of healthy personality, psychology has undertaken full responsibility for a task that is essentially religious and has attempted to do so purely on the level of the natural. If, in the present examination, it is discovered that psychology and Christianity do not always coincide, and that psychology fails miserably in face of the nature of the task at hand, it would appear that this work has, to some extent, been justified.

The chapters which follow present an intentional progression. Chapters in Part I are intended to pave the way for further discussions by bringing certain broad controversial issues to attention and recasting them in the light of Christian teaching. In Parts II and III, several models are constructed and utilized to explicate the developing person and to indicate where psychology and Christianity, as defined here, meet and where they are at odds one with the other on the subject of personal development. No restrictions are placed on the discussion in that a look at both healthy and unhealthy development is attempted to varying degrees. Part IV deals more extensively with selected disparities between Christianity and present-day psychology, indicating their incompatibilities and treating them to critical analysis.

PART I

CLEARING THE UNDER-GROWTH:

THE CASE AGAINST UNBELIEF

1. Controversial Issues

It is a serious thing when an individual misses his true calling in life—that task or vocation for which he seems to have been fitted with special aptitudes and which he could have executed with a certain native ease. It is a more serious thing when an individual fails to become the person he was meant to be—to present his particular facade in the kaleidoscope of "mankind made in the image of God," and thereby fails to glorify his Maker as he ought. It is the most serious mistake for a man to fail to take the Lord Jesus Christ as his Model, Guide, Redeemer, Friend in his struggle to become a person, for in Christ *"dwelleth all the fullness of the Godhead bodily"* (Colossians 2:9). He is the only perfect example of human personhood.

Today, the greatest irony within psychology, the science of human behaviour and personality, is that it ignores the only Person who can impart full personality. Psychology itself is not bereft of heroes and heroines. Its exponents (notably Maslow, Fowler, etc.) have lauded personages like Mahatma Gandhi, Eleanor Roosevelt, Martin Luther King and Mother Teresa who are considered to have attained the pinnacle of personality in the form of self-actualization. Psychology invites the contemplation of far-fetched ideologies, philosophies and social forms of religion; it establishes humanism as an alternative religion, replete with creed and manifesto; it promotes forms of transcendental meditation geared to resolve nervous tensions and believed to be the panacea for personality disorders; it speaks shyly of ecumenism, world unity and the transformation of human personality; but nowhere is there a full-blown theory which introduces Christianity as the context of true personality development and the Christ of Christianity as the Giver.

It is not that psychology is intrinsically and wholly irreligious. There are theories of personality which have significant religious overtones; but the religious components of theories of personality, where they exist, are largely humanistic, neutral, half-hearted and lacking in outspoken conviction regarding the divine source of personality. Some few theories have even been associated with the supernatural in inspiration and in content, but this influence has almost exclusively been restricted to the satanic or the quasi-satanic. The general problem is that psychology, properly viewed, has undeniable religious implications but these are studiously excised or given biased and selective treatment. The specific problem is that psychology is devitalized, de-vitaminized, dehydrated and dimidiated.

How has this come about? It was not by accident. The embarrassingly secular presentation in psychological theory is not due to the nature of man, nor is it a necessity as we have been encouraged to believe by most of the leading psychological journals today. The largely atheistic and more specifically non-Christian character of psychological theory in today's world is due to a simple artifact of the modern age—the lack of Christian conviction among the many illustrious names which represent the "big theorists."

Psychology, since the 1930s, has become a closed loop. The tight circle of atheistic or agnostic thinkers have, so to speak, seen to it—either tacitly or by design—that the science of psychology is severed from any reference to the Christian gospel. Associations like the APA have, not without loss, discouraged publication of any endeavour which sought to explain personality in Christian terms. It is only in recent years that periodicals like the *Journal of Psychology and Christianity* have come into being. Nor was this lack of deference for the Christian faith a closed secret. It was openly acknowledged by the leading personality theorists themselves. Carl Rogers, whose theory has influenced millions of people, some because of his alleged early tendencies towards the religious and his devout family background, was in fact a religious liberalist in the later years of his life![1] Carl Jung, so impressive a figure for the psychological novitiate, is not always known to have been a man absorbed with the occult and with mediums, who conversed with voices from within his psyche, including a female that he interpreted as his "anima," a wise old man, and a group of ghosts he believed to be souls returning from the dead.[2] Very few today seem to know that B.F. Skinner, the renowned behaviourist, was among the signatories of the Humanist Manifesto II in 1973 and as such presented humanism, this "high-minded, science-oriented ethic" as an alternative and innocuous religion, claiming that human beings are at the center of the universe and maintaining that nature, with man at the zenith, is all that exists.

It is not surprising then that the main issues in theories of psychology seem to follow a systematic secular bias. It is ironic, however, that the end result of this bias is an extreme dogmatism which manages somehow to survive in a scientific system which prefers to describe reality as democratic and relativistic. That is, although psychologists in general renounce the existence of absolutes and promote belief in the relativity of truth and of values, the exclusivity with which this is done denies their own avowed intent.

The major theme of this section, to be developed later, is the profound conviction that the erroneous foundation on which most of psychology is built has led to many fallacious arguments and propositions. The positions taken habitually with respect to numerous controversial issues have not only confused our understanding of human personality but have left many more specific questions in personality theory hopelessly unanswered. An attempt will be made, in the ensuing paragraphs, to analyze three major controversial issues and to shed light on them by subjecting them to the illumination of the Christian gospel. The way will thus be opened for other weaknesses in personality theory to be examined carefully.

THE NATURE OF ULTIMATE REALITY

This question has been tossed about in one way or another by every philosopher who ever lived. Philosophy has engaged countless questions ranging from the metaphysical ("Where have I come from?" "Where am I going?" etc.) to the ontological ("Who am I?" etc.) to the epistemological questions ("What do I know?" "How do I know that I know?" "What is the origin of knowledge?" etc.). It is not always in the nature of philosophy to provide answers to questions. Like the child, the philosopher is good at interrogation but often cares little for the answer. Like jesting Pilot, referred to in Bacon's essays, he asks, "What is truth?" but does not stay for an answer. Perhaps the answers will not be provided by philosophy but by faith.

The question regarding the nature of ultimate reality will, perhaps, enjoy a similar fate. It is not only ancient in origin but it is so germane to the interests of every thinker that it provides a recurrent, or more accurately, a stable theme in philosophy. It has been repeated in every age, with no exceptions, since man's earliest recollection. It is a question which, though it has evoked numberless suggestions as answers, can best be discussed under two general headings: the theocentric and anthropocentric points of view.

THEOCENTRISM

Theocentrism, as distinct from deism (based on reason and rejecting supernatural revelation and care), is the belief—held largely by Christians, Jews and Muslims—in a self-revelatory God who, as Creator, loves, cares for and is present to His creation, abiding in them at their invitation but totally independent of their existence as creatures (see Isaiah 40:1-31). This personal God is Supreme Being, far above all else.

> *Be still and know that I am God: I will be exalted among the heathen, I will be exalted in the earth* (Psalm 46:10).

To the theist, reality is God. There is no other answer to the age-old philosophical debate on the nature of ultimate reality.

Nowhere is this answer better portrayed than in the effusive but eloquent discourse given by the philosopher St. Paul to his Athenian colleagues at Mars Hill in the first century AD. Confronted by their unbelief, he declared the concept—new to them and, unfortunately, as new today in many quarters—that:

> *God that made the world and all things therein, seeing that he is Lord of heaven and earth, dwelleth not in temples made with hands; Neither is worshipped with men's hands, as though he needed any thing, seeing he giveth to all life, and breath, and all things;... For in him we live, and move, and have our being...* (Acts 17:24-25,28).

God, who is not withdrawn from His creation but is totally independent of it, shows His graciousness in Jesus Christ. For the Christian, it is possible for the human being to develop a relationship with God through grace—God's riches given at Christ's expense. The Christian accepts God's redeeming grace, His saving grace, His keeping grace, His healing grace.

> *The Spirit of the Lord is upon me, because he hath anointed me to preach the gospel to the poor; he hath sent me to heal the broken-hearted, to preach deliverance to the captives, and recovering of sight to the blind, to set at liberty them that are bruised, To preach the acceptable year of the Lord* (Luke 4:18,19).

> *To appoint unto them that mourn in Zion, to give unto them beauty for ashes, the oil of joy for mourning...* (Isaiah 61:3).

Christian theism takes the view that spirit surpasses the intellect or mind and describes the highest level of reality. Spirit is closer to the heart than it is to our intellectual mind and thereby expresses our essence more clearly. When man is indwelt by the Spirit of God, *"It is the spirit that quickeneth; the flesh profiteth nothing"* (John 6:63). In dealing with God, the criterion is never the opinionated self nor fortune nor fame but relationship with God, for in this way there is always parity and there is always equity.

ANTHROPOCENTRISM

The anthropocentric point of view promotes man. It sees man as being at the center of the universe. This may take one of many forms.

The ancient Greeks of the second century, led by Ptolemy, interpreted our astronomical system to mean that the earth was the central body around which the sun, planets and all other celestial bodies revolved. Since man inhabited this planet, it had to be the centerpiece. This early form of anthropocentrism was restricted to the physical/material aspect of reality. The breakaway occurred in the early sixteenth century when the Polish scientist, Copernicus (1473-1543), exploded this belief and pronounced that the earth and other planets revolve about the sun. This later view, displacing the earth from the central position given it in the Ptolemaic system, was supported by Galileo (1564-1642). Though the material form of anthropocentrism has been shattered and has been disproved many times, other forms have never really been displaced.

Humanism, put in its simplest terms, is a declaration that man is to be exalted. The humanist is pro man. Whether we examine the early humanism of the ancient Greeks with its idolization of human virtues and intellectual excellence, or the Enlightenment humanism of the eighteenth century when men responded once again to the ancient call for reason, or the Romantic humanism of the nineteenth century given to passion and to vanity, the position remains essentially the same.

The effort is made to place man at the pinnacle of existence and to glorify him. Even the Renaissance humanism of the sixteenth century, perhaps a feeble hymn of worship to the Creator, seems overpowered with the zeal for Greek art and sculpture—the works of man's hands—rather than zeal for the submission of his heart! Finally, the secular humanism of the twentieth century has been referred to by many as merely a neo-anthropocentric point of view; this time not physical in import but psychological.

The anthropocentric orientation, best illustrated by the humanistic persuasion which troubles so much of our twentieth century ideology, denounces the supremacy of the Godhead. It turns to man for purpose, for method, for questions and for answers. In dealing with the question of the nature of ultimate reality, the answer of the humanist may be supported, even today, by two classic doctrines in ancient philosophy: realism and idealism.

Realism

Aristotle (384-322 BC), as the earliest known and perhaps the most open-minded proponent of realism, took the view that ultimate reality subsists in matter or that which may be experienced through the senses. The central tenet of realism or the thesis of *independence*, holds, in essence, that reality, knowledge and value exist independently of the human mind. The realist asserts, as fact, that the actual sticks, stones and trees of the universe exist whether or not there is a human mind to perceive them. Aristotle himself, however, was too broad-minded to accept the limitations of this statement. He recognized the important role of reason in the acquisition of truth. Unfortunately, according to Aristotle, reason was basically the mental capacity to make associations, similar to the behaviouristic laws of twentieth-century psychologists (laws of contiguity, similarity, etc.). He did not emphasize the more sophisticated cognitive interpretation of reason as the ability to achieve understanding and insight. Unfortunately, too, Aristotle did not appreciate that "the heart has its reasons which the reason knows nothing of" (Blaise Pascal, *Pensees*).

Aristotelian realism persisted through the centuries. It propounded the belief that, while ideas may be important in themselves, a proper study of matter as contrasted to the study of ideas, could lead us to better and more distinct ideas. Each piece of matter has both a *universal* (e.g. the acorn's "acornness") and a *particular* aspect (e.g. the size, colour, weight of the acorn). Both humanness and acornness are realities and they exist independently and regardless of any one human or acorn, but they can best be studied by the examination of the particular human or acorn.

The realist position taken by Aristotle led to the educational approach known as empiricism, favoured by modern theorists such as John Dewey, B.F. Skinner and Albert Bandura.

Idealism

Generally, idealists believe that ideas, not matter, are the only true reality. The word "idea-ism" may therefore be a more correct descriptive term for this philosophy than the word "idealism." Idealism was birthed in the cradle of the Socratic dialectical method. Plato (427-347 BC) was its chief literary proponent in ancient Greece. For the idealist, the world of ideas is the source of all true knowledge. The world of matter, with its ever-changing sensory data, is not therefore to be trusted. To attain the Good, matter must be transcended through the use of the dialectic. In Plato's *Republic*, the philosopher king has no interest in materialism, nor even in the act of ruling itself. He rules because he must, because as a philosopher, he is the best suited for the task. The idealist does not believe in a personal God. The nature of his god is basically Mind or Self. The idealist god is the self-conscious unity of all reality. To the idealist, man's bridge to ultimate reality is the mind.

Idealism, fostered by later philosophers such as Descartes, Berkeley, Kant and Hegel, has encouraged the educational methods known as mentalism, structuralism and recently, cognitivism. Usually, the idealist position is that the pupil is a transcendental self who needs to be freed from the fetters of the physical and social world. Mind or self is primary. It could be said, then, that both idealism and realism, void of any emphasis on theism, are largely supportive of present-day humanism. Since Greek idealism and realism were the natural precursors to present-day cognitivism and behaviourism respectively, it is perhaps fair to deduce that at some level of conceptualization, all three major schools of thought in psychology, that is, humanism, cognitivism and behaviourism are essentially humanist in character and thus anthropocentric, either by intention or by default.

To the Judeo-Christian, unlike any of the anthropocentric positions just described, ultimate reality is God and our bridge to Him is not the mind but the heart. Christian theism presents a reality which is quite different from that of the natural world or of anything learned purely by the senses. It is not the reality of matter, nor is it the "other reality" depicted by Plato in his allegory of the cave. It is not the reality of self-conscious unity or of mind. It is, rather, the reality of the spirit. It is the reality of a world where death, should it occur, is more horrendous than material decay. Man, made in the image of God and a potential participant in the world of spirit or life, is essentially comprised of body, soul and spirit. Spirit, as the dominant disposition or his immaterial essence, involves the nurturing of faith which is the vehicle of the spirit. In humble recognition of her human limitations in attempting to define spirit, the author suggests that spirit transcends mind for, while it involves the character of the mind, it is the capacity of the whole person buttressed by desire for devotion. This having been said, the author later rejoiced to come across the following quotation:

> The spirit in man, therefore, is that transcendent capacity whereby man, grasping himself totally in an act of decisive commitment may relate himself to God as person to Person (S.R. Hopper, "The Crisis of Faith," in H. Maloney, *A Christian Existential Psychology*).

For the Christian this means devotion to Christ as Lord and is the result of the work of the Holy Spirit Himself who engages the heart of the individual. In this way the concepts of spirit, mind and heart are intricately dovetailed without necessarily being synonymous.

The educational approach adopted by the Christian theist then, must be primarily centered on faith in Jesus Christ. Faith involves not only belief but also the submission of the will, obedience, love and loyalty. This is the only answer for the Christian for whom the issues of life revolve around Christ. This "seed," as the basis for psychological theory on human development, has been planted and watered but has encountered setbacks and, although germinated, the sapling has not yet taken root. Like the seed in the parable of the Master, there was no depth of earth and in places where the sapling should be nurtured, there has been dissembling.

For those who claim to be Christian, the adoption of an educational approach that panders principally to humanistic psychology is contradictory and self-defeating. Many have been tempted to do this. There is too much evidence of it in our educational psychology textbooks which offer limp implications for the theories they describe. There is even more evidence in our schools where we wave the banner of the Christian but teach the standards of the humanist, creating the monster of personal, ethical, moral and religious confusion. The usual reasoning is that the humanist is basically a "spiritual" person, aspiring to heightened expression of self-actualization,[3] of service to the community and of healthy interpersonal relationship. So far so good. This argument proves, however, to be specious. Humanistic psychology, when summarized by Ansbacher,[4] presents the following six basic premises:

1. man's creative power as a crucial force, in addition to heredity and environment
2. an anthropomorphic instead of a mechanomorphic model of man
3. the teleological concept of purpose, rather than cause, as the decisive dynamic in personality
4. the holistic approach to the study of man as more adequate than the elementaristic one
5. the necessity of taking man's subjectivity, his opinions and viewpoints, conscious and unconscious, fully into account
6. psychotherapy as essentially based on a good human relationship

These premises served to unite all those included by Maslow in his "third force" or "humanistic" psychology, that is, the Adlerians, representatives of personalism (Allport), the original Gestalt school, and existentialists; the neo-Freudians (Eric

Fromm, Karen Horney, H.S. Sullivan), the phenomenologists, the Rogerians and George Kelly.

Nowhere in the six premises stated above, however, nor in the works of those who shared these premises, do we find a trace of explicit commitment to spirituality which rises above that on the natural/social level. While the six previous tenets serve to lift man above the level of the animal or the mundane, they do nothing to place him in the category of "man made in the image of God" to have fellowship with Him. On the contrary, one may suspect after a while that the humanist regards himself as having arrived without the conversion experience and the redemptive work of Christ.

The true Christian understands the fallacies behind the humanist position. It should be recognized that in the Christianity of the early Church, religion can never be subordinate to the social. Further, Christians of the twentieth century should realize that, since by definition and by allegiance to the Person whose name they adopt, they must be theistic, the goals, ideas and essence of humanism are discrepant with their faith. For the Christian, God, who is ultimate reality, is much too great to be contained by the works of mankind's hands.

RELATIVES VERSUS ABSOLUTES

> The Modern Age, more or less repudiating the idea of a divine lawgiver, has nevertheless tried to retain the ideas of moral right and wrong, not noticing that, in casting God aside, they have also abolished the conditions of meaningfulness for moral right and wrong... (R. Taylor, *Ethics, Faith and Reason*).

It would seem that our modern age is the age of relativism and situationalism. It is not difficult to see why. Empiricism, which claims that truth can be known only through experience, is firmly established. But since we cannot all have the same experience, truth, discovered by this means, must remain relative. In 1980, H. Newton Malony described the scientific dilemma this way:

> ...as more and more scientists (to name only Michael Polanyi) are observing, so-called scientific objectivity has long been exploded as a myth. It is ironic: Physical scientists treat their methodology with tongue-in-cheek, fully aware of its serious limitations—while psychologists, who are social scientists, are still very dedicated to this method (*A Christian Existential Psychology*).

The difficulty is that science and its methods, which have captured our imagination and our respect in recent decades, have proven to be a great deal more subjective than they were previously thought to be. Scientists, like psychologists, are at heart essentially philosophers and, as such, will never approximate truth unless they are willing to relinquish more of their subjectivity. In the meantime, we suffer from the fallibility of the scientific approach and the heady assumptions which are often ingrained in its hypotheses. Men, for example, no longer stop to look critically at the theory of evolution and to wonder whether Darwin was indeed correct. By and large, entire nations and cultures have assumed that evolution is true though it still is only a theory supported by a finite number of pieces of evidence and an equal number of contradictions.

When the thralldom to science becomes intolerable by the overwhelming evidence both for and against the truth of a given proposition, humanism perpetuates the practice of relativism. The humanistic attitude usually is that mankind is self-sufficient and promisingly enterprising in the struggle for a new world order; since, however, each person and each group has the right to be individualistic, truth must once again be relative to the situation and to the preferences of those within it.

Some of this is no doubt valid and inescapable. Our human history is consistent in demonstrating that very often the exigencies of the situation make it absolutely necessary to apply relative truths in the solution to a problem. Somewhere, however, among the many billion relatives that exist in our world, there are perhaps an equal number of absolutes. These must be extricated, collated, sifted and sorted. No one need look very far to find absolutes. In spite of scientific effort to halt the course of life by freezing either the foetus or the full-grown individual, it is a self-evident truth that every man must die. In physics, it is an accepted fact that if certain two gases meet, there must be an explosion. On the level of the spiritual and the supernatural, it is equally evident to the enlightened that each man must be "born again" if he is to escape spiritual death. Likewise, in absolute terms, we are told that *"whosoever will"*(Revelation 22:17) may come.

In the realm of dialectics, it may be posited that there can be no relative truths, no small "t's," unless there is, somewhere, a big "T," an absolute upon which to base the comparatives and from which their essence may be derived. Likewise, the meaning of the situational truth cannot be understood without reference to a standard or an absolute. Neither will reason, nor its companion, experience, suffice as a basis for the truth since these, too, are relative depending on the perception of the individual. Pure logic, which is admirably suited to the manipulation of words, is not at all adequate in the case of real needs and problems. It is a well-known fact that a statement may adhere absolutely to formal logic and yet be utterly untrue or even nonsensical. We are left forcibly, then, with the necessity to decide, by some other means, which truths we will take as absolutes if only to help us get along with the relatives that often obstruct our way.

The task of finding absolutes for their own sake and because of their own truth value is more than interesting. It is human to answer the compelling call to do so. Every living human being does so, whether implicitly or explicitly, whether consciously or unknowingly, whether intentionally or by implication. Without these convictions we cannot live. Indeed, the person who can make no sense of life and who enjoys no glimmer of truth is the person who becomes insane. By extension, it is fair to say that those who prattle against the existence of absolutes must have either a greater endowment of provocative tolerance for doubt or a perverted need to prove that there are none.

Obviously, then, there is a universal human dilemma. There is a human need to discover the existence of absolutes but the need can neither be supplied by fallible reason nor by limited experience. Fortunately for us there is a third option—that of revelation and faith. When revelation is supported not only by faith but also by experience, it is all the more exciting.

The Christian believes through revelation and bears witness experientially to the fact that God is love. The absolute love of the Divine is matched by His absolute justice and preceded by His holiness. God alone is absolute. This springs from His omniscience, His omnipotence and His omnipresence. Human beings speak of justice but they are ill-equipped to practise it through lack of knowledge and of love. The love of man-to-man, though serenaded, is always tainted and conditional. God's love alone is limitless in its outreach, infinite in its inclusiveness and perfect in its expression. God's judgment, however, is also relative. Though His justice is absolute, His judgment is relative to our understanding and our experience of revelation. "The paradox of final revelation, overcoming the conflict between absolutism and relativism, is Love..." (Paul Tillich, *Systematic Theology*).

The best example of God's absolute love is His expression of love to us in Christ Jesus: *"God so loved the world that he gave his only begotten Son..."* (John 3:16). This belief does not rest merely on hearsay but on first-hand experience. It is not sparked by reason but by faith. But having been so sparked, there is an effective union between the relative reason and the absolute faith: *"Said I not unto thee, that, if thou wouldest believe, thou shouldest see the glory of God?"* (John 11:40).

Why should psychologists persist in dethroning and disbarring such absolute Beauty?

THE NATURE OF MAN - GOOD, BAD OR NEUTRAL?

In psychology, where it may be said that this discussion is confined to the nature of natural man, there are varying opinions in four outstanding schools of thought—psychoanalysis, behaviourism, cognitivism and humanism.

Psychoanalysis

Psychoanalysis, without a doubt, presents man as bad. Life, death and sex instincts are characterized as primitive libidinal drives of the *id* which is subject to passions and tainted by perversions. For neo-psychoanalysts, development of the entire personality is considered to be based on the maturity of specific psychosexual zones, complemented by equally specific psychosocial modalities. Though Freud's assessment is severe and his explanation of personality is one-sided, his remarks are not altogether unsound. Apart from the miraculous transformation possible only through the grace of God, what Freud says about the luridness of human nature is often every bit true. It is reechoed by St. Paul (Romans 1:24-26 and Galatians 5:19-21). Where Freud was at fault was in his putting greater emphasis on man's sexual lusts. He forgot all the other lusts of the flesh—pride, envy, hatred...

The problem of evil in man's nature—so starkly represented by Freud—is equally well understood by Rollo May, whose evaluation of man is so austere that few in the humanistic climate of the 1980s and 1990s will agree with him:

> The culture is evil as well as good because we, the human beings who constitute it, are evil as well as good. Our culture is partially destructive because we, as human beings who live in it, are partially destructive, whether we be Russians or Japanese or Germans or Americans ("The Problem of Evil: An Open Letter to Carl Rogers," in Kirschenbaum and Henderson, *Carl Rogers: Dialogues*).

COGNITIVISM AND BEHAVIOURISM

In spite of their polarized positions on many issues, two psychological schools of thought, cognitivism and behaviourism, both argue that the nature of man is neither good nor bad, but neutral. The usual approach, subject to minor modifications, is to suggest that man is neither the master of his destiny nor the captain of his fate and is shaped by the environment in which he finds himself whether it is hostile and malevolent or benign and nurturing.

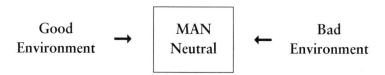

The assumption is that the outcome for man, lacking in substantive character of his own, depends entirely on the forces of the environment. If the good forces outweigh the bad, man will be secure, tending to reflect the salutary nature of the environment. If the bad forces are in the ascendancy, however, man will pay the penalty, himself becoming infected with the malignity of the virus.

There are a number of flaws in this position. First, the cognitivists who take this view are momentarily unmindful of those among them—for example the social learning theorist, Bandura,[5]—who have painstakingly shown that the environment can hardly be totally responsible for a particular proclivity. Bandura accomplishes this by emphasizing his concept of "reciprocal determinism." At the moment of any given interaction, there is already a residue of the qualitative environment within the person himself who is acting on the environment. Likewise, there is already a significant reflection of the person himself in the environment as it acts on him. The individual represented within the box of the preceding graphic, therefore, is never a totally intact entity. When we encounter him, he has already drunk at the pool for weal or for woe, and muddied the waters in the process. At any given point in time, the environment probably owes as much to the individual as the individual owes to the environment.

An argument which is even more damaging to the "neutral position" is the fact that, in a discussion on the nature of generic mankind, there really is no "environment" with which to contend. If the situation is properly appraised, we find that the so-called "environment" is a mixed bag comprised of input by other human beings. The hostility to which most psychologists refer is not that of the capricious weather; it is not the slow but obtrusive encroachment of the desert as it swallows more arable land; nor is it the frigidity of the "concrete jungle" with its depersonalized architecture, its steely miles of swirling highway and its monstrous inner cities sometimes only a shell, a ghost town; nor is it the foamy seas and spear-like rocks in the straits betwixt Charybdis and Scylla paralleled by the dangers of the Bermuda Triangle. It is, ironically, the hostility of the other man, or of seething hordes of angry men feeling their hurt. Was it the environment that brought about the Los Angeles riots in 1992, or was it man's inhumanity to man? The Californian incident is not atypical, for this is happening all over the world.

In such a circumstance, if we use the environment as a scapegoat, we find ourselves with precisely the same question with which we began—"What is man?"

If we are discussing man, then, to be honest we must get the environment out of the way, whatever its nature. We must exonerate it if necessary.

Perhaps the most serious point to be made is that, in accepting the argument that man's nature is neutral, man is allowed to abdicate his responsibility. The gardner does not give up his rights to enjoy the benefits of the garden but he also does everything to improve it, to maintain it. Further, he must not be allowed, having drunk at the spring, to foul it for posterity. Every individual must therefore, not only be invested with rights and privileges but must also be invested with responsibility. While a thing, *per se*, may be neutral, its character being entirely dependent on the use to which it is put, no person can be neutral by nature unless he is simultaneously irresponsible. Neutrality simply cannot be maintained if man is considered to be the highest form of intelligence on the earth. Although the argument that man is neutral has attractions and would provide a route of escape, we must reject it as spurious.

Finally, we need to be wary of the word "neutral." It does not merely mean innocuous. Rather, it has implications regarding man's character, or lack thereof, which are often not understood.

Humanism

Man's alleged goodness has been defended largely by humanism, the school of thought spearheaded by Rousseau, Rogers and Maslow, which holds that human ideals and the perfection of human personality are central, so that cultural and practical interests rather than theology and metaphysics are in the focus of attention. It is interesting to note, just at this point, that the derivation of the English word "good" is the old English "gōd." Does the case for the prosecution rest with the simple assertion, *"There is none good but one, that is, God"* (Matthew 19:17).

Humanism's most pervasive problem, next to its presumptuousness and pride, is its failure to deal adequately with the very present problem of evil in the world. The humanist persists in pronouncing men good even though all the evidence is against this. The feeble excuse is often "evil is what you make it." Another favourite escape hatch is the declaration that "though man is not perfect, he is still good."

The objective onlooker will probably agree that it is time for the humanist to stop deceiving himself. Man's desperate need to love himself does not make self-flattery any less destructive. Humanism's deception has persisted for so long that it has invited decadence. Humanism is now being described as a contagious case of "neo-narcissism." America's leading existentialist, Rollo May, had this to say about humanism:

> The issue of evil—or rather, the issue of not confronting evil—has profound, and to my mind adverse, effects on

humanistic psychology... humanistic psychology is the narcissism of our culture... the narcissists are persons who are turned inward rather than outward, who are so lost in self-love that they cannot see and relate to the reality outside themselves, including other human beings ("The Problem of Evil: an open letter to Carl Rogers," in Kirschenbaum and Henderson, *Carl Rogers: Dialogues*).

This statement, directed at the very school of thought which once declared its proponents free of the narcissism portrayed in Freudian psychology, is no compliment.

It does not take much imagination to understand that if a right angle is defined as an angle of ninety degrees, then any angle which deviates from this, no matter how fractionally, is not a right angle. Similarly, if good is defined as perfect, upright, adequate, wholesome, then any departure from this, no matter how infinitesimal, cannot be good. The burning question which needs to be asked of those who still defend humanism's hope in man's goodness is simply this—show us the goodness in man; does it measure up? If man is so good, why is it that he does not consistently resist the evil environment? Indeed, if man is good, presumably including those in the environment, where did the first evil in the world come from?

The intellectual debate around the issue of man's presumed goodness is focused largely on the theories of the three humanist giants—Rousseau[6], Rogers[7] and Maslow.[8] For Rousseau, the root of evil is civilization. The young fictional hero of his novel, Emile, is a paragon of virtue who bears an intuitive sense of the good and is guided by it. If he is allowed to spend his days in the cloistered sanctuary of the rural world, he will continue to be virtuous and to achieve his full potential. If, on the other hand, he is exposed to the decadence of the urban environment, he will deteriorate morally in time. In this event, the blame is not attached to Emile but to the noxious environment of which he is a part. Emile, to all intents and purposes, remains good at heart.

This Romantic humanism of Rousseau, otherwise known as Romantic naturalism, must have weighed heavily on Rogers, creating a tremendous influence on his writing. Although Rogers realizes the great human capacity for cruel and destructive behaviour, he does not hold man responsible. He attributes this primarily to the environment. The reason adduced by Rogers is that the most fundamental levels of personality are inherently positive since we have a tendency to actualize our benign inner potentials. Should evil occur, then, it is excused on the ground that circumstantial blocks caused us to behave in ways that belie our benign inner nature. The astute reader will judge for himself.

Abraham Maslow, recognized as a contemporary exponent of humanism, is, in many ways, of the same mind as Rogers. Maslow believes that our inner needs (both deficiency and being needs), described as "innate instinctoid tendencies," are predominantly healthy and benign, giving us an inherent capacity for positive growth. There is, however, one redeeming feature in his thought, one basic difference between himself and Rogers. Whereas Rogers is persistently sold out on the idea of man's basic goodness, Maslow acknowledges that our basic needs for safety, belonging and love, esteem and self-actualization are "instinct-remnants" which are weak and very easily overwhelmed by the more powerful forces of learning and culture.

> The human needs... are weak and feeble rather than unequivocal and unmistakable; they whisper rather than shout. And the whisper is easily drowned out (A.H. Maslow, *Motivation and Personality*).

The result is that a pathogenic environment can easily be detrimental to our imperfect human nature, inhibiting positive potentials and evoking self-destructiveness. Maslow is not saying here that the environment is so remarkably destructive. What he is saying is that the human being is so terribly weak. This includes all people. For Maslow, even the self-actualizing person is not perfect.

The best that can be said of the humanistic approach is that those who take recourse in the belief in the alleged goodness of man must immediately admit that something bad happened to him "on the way to the forum," that he lost his clothes and the integrity with which he was putatively credited.

None of the four major psychological schools has dealt adequately with the problem of evil. In contemplating humanism, it becomes obvious that the need man has to see himself as good and the recognition of evil in his nature become an absurd contradiction unless they are reconciled.

THE CHRISTIAN VIEW

It would seem that in any discussion of the nature of generic man, that is, man taken as a universal species, it will not be long before our purist aspirations become cluttered by reference to the many types of human beings that exist. Categories will slip easily, undetected at first, into the field being surveyed. They cannot, however, be usefully eliminated from the discussion. They must therefore be dealt with as potential dialectical humbugs by keeping them in their correct place within the larger scheme. Not to retain the lines of demarcation would render the arguments confused, circular and self-defeating. It is therefore necessary to set up the parameters and limitations for the discussion by constructing a model. Only then can we justifiably introduce our monumental question.

The model in Figure 1 attempts a comprehensive set of categories relative to the Christian perspective of man. Basic to the model is the premise that human beings live either in the realm of the natural (represented by the space within the inner circle), exercising strengths and skills which are natural endowments, or in the realm of the supernatural (represented by the space between the two circles), influenced by and subject to relationship with supernatural powers.

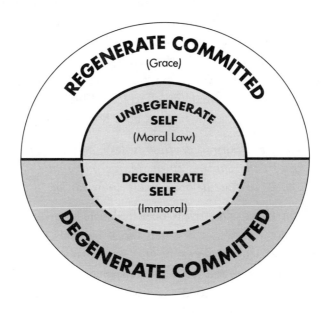

Figure 1 - THE NATURE OF MAN

In the latter realm we come up against two categories as different as the poles are asunder and it is necessary to put up a road sign of caution lest we slip on ignorance. In the former realm, there is no firm decisive line between the two categories, both being located within the kingdom of evil, represented by the shaded area. The Law instructs. It also condemns. Ultimately, the model presents only two kingdoms or two powers pertinent to the experience of the human being—the Kingdom of God and the kingdom under the sway of satanic powers.

The first and highest of the four major categories, "Regenerate Committed," refers to the person who, through faith in Jesus Christ, has come into relationship with God and is fully under His control. He is living in a state of grace. In this condition he will undoubtedly bear fruit unto God. He does not depend, however, on his own righteousness for salvation but solely on the righteousness of Christ (Galations 5:4).

The second category, "Unregenerate Self," denotes the person who attempts to live a good life subject to the moral law but who has not submitted himself to Jesus Christ. This person is unregenerate because he has not been born again.

> *That which is born of the flesh is flesh; and that which is born of the Spirit is spirit. Marvel not that I said unto thee, Ye must be born again* (John 3:6,7).

This person will usually strive to obey the law in his own strength, therefore, not realizing at first that this is humanly impossible. When he does achieve success on the lesser matters, he will discover that he has missed the mark somewhere in respect to the weightier matters. The "good" man who cares for his neighbour may suddenly realize he has been motivated by pride. The unregenerate self is admittedly not perfect, but neither is it good, for all its striving. In the eyes of God, the person is outside His grace. The practising humanist is included in this category.

The "Degenerate Self" denotes the type who has little or no moral intent. The person's orientation is toward evil rather than good. Basic immorality, not pursuing that which is known to be good, leads to inevitable degeneracy. Like the unregenerate self, this person lives only on the level of the natural—the self or nature—without any consideration of the supernatural. Being wrapped in the self, there is a foregone exclusion of God. Unlike the unregenerate self, however, there is no apparent caring for one's neighbour.

The type "Degenerate Committed," though completing the cycle of those who aspire to relationship with the supernatural, is placed at the lowest level of the model representing satanic allegiance and therefore the pit of human experience.

The dual orientations towards the kingdoms of good versus evil basic to the model require further explanation. In keeping with biblical terminology, "flesh" is coterminous with an orientation towards evil. That is, the term flesh is also used to describe the unregenerate self who strives but fails and continues to rely on native effort.

> *For I know that in me (that is, in my flesh,) dwelleth no good thing: for to will is present with me; but how to perform that which is good I find not* (Romans 7:18).

We are also instructed—*"Walk in the Spirit, and ye shall not fulfil the lusts of the flesh"* (Galatians 5:16).

The most striking distinction, therefore, in the entire model is that between Regenerate Man on the one hand, and the remaining three categories on the other hand. In effect, the discussion will revolve primarily around two groups, man actuated by the Spirit versus man actuated by the flesh. It was thought to be more prudent to attempt this dichotomy rather than to retain the natural/supernatural realms as the dividing line. It was envisaged that the latter division would only have led to confusion since there is no one-to-one correspondence, according to the model, between good versus evil and the supernatural versus the natural.

When the two most salient categories—man walking in the Spirit versus man walking in the flesh—have been fully described and discussed, an attempt will be made to see if an observation on the nature of generic man may be made.

Man Actuated by the Flesh

The picture of man outside the experience of regeneration—the man of "flesh"—is a motley one. The spirit has been bypassed and has been subjected to a total eclipse. Having become aware of the mind, man has consistently endeavoured to idolize the power which comes from this source, not realizing that this pursuit is fetid and always leads to a cul-de-sac. The Authority on this subject says, *"It is the spirit that quickeneth; the flesh profiteth nothing"* (John 6:63). While the Lighthouse seeks to deter him from following the flesh, he discards the warning and the beaches are full of wrecks cast up by the waves.

Man has built many empires, destroyed as many and probed the nearest fringes of outer space. In doing so, he has demonstrated the potency of his mind. Yet, for all this, his thinking, for much of the time, remains very ordinary, subject to mistakes, misunderstandings and serious errors. When confronted with the cold evidence of his misconceptions, it is dismissed by the adage *errare humana est*. Philosophy and psychology have encouraged rhetoric, developed dialectic and given birth to numerous schools of thought. Sometimes, as the philosopher continues, eyes cast down, to study and upturn the earthy mud, he stumbles on veins of gold hidden here and there: man-made theories infused with pride and unbelief. Without submitting them to the Refiner, he wears them as dull metal, for the mud which still encases the ore never shines as true gold. The veins unearthed are disconnected, packed with heavy clod, impure, unpolished. Neither philosophy nor psychology has brought the solutions to life. Rather, they have served only to illustrate the aggravating fallibility and weakness of the best of minds and the need for a heavenly Metallurgist. Behaviouristic experimentalism and behaviour modification theory among others, when seriously applied in educational settings, have shuffled mountains by inches. Yet the miracles achieved here leave murky clouds of trailing dust hanging heavily over the landscape.

The mind of natural man attempts to rule itself. In too many cases, absolutes have been dethroned. The mind's prime target has been the overthrow of the highest Absolute, its Maker. In his egoism, egocentrism and pride, modern man has substituted himself, rather, his mind, as the centre of the universe. But man was not made to exalt himself. He was not made for prejudice and pride. He was made to reflect the *imago Dei*, to worship Him who "made us for Himself, (because) …our souls can find no rest until we rest at peace with Him" (St. Augustine, *City of God*).

All our difficulty begins with pride. It was pride that dislodged the Evil One, the Angel of Light, from his heavenly abode and caused him to be removed from his post, hurtled out of Heaven and consigned to everlasting exile. It was lust for power and pride that marred the young creation. It was arrogance that led to carelessness and ultimate defeat in each succeeding civilization of the world—that of the Greeks, the Romans, the Carthaginians and even the promise of Constantine's Constantinople. It was vanity, pride of life, lust of the eyes, lust of the flesh that bred self-consciousness, the antipathy of God-consciousness, anger, hatred, carnality, selfishness, variance, unholy introspection… Satan's temptation, *"All this power will I give…"* is still ugly.

The mind of natural man attempts to prove itself. It also claims to be the last frontier in the realm of his existence. Currently, psychobiology and biochemistry applied to the study of the brain are expected by some[9] to be the last word in understanding our human condition. The brain is admittedly the seat of physical as well as neurophysiological activity. As the alleged basis of the mind it has also been interpreted as the power-house of intuition, biofeedback and the blueprint for personality types (left-brain dominance produces, it is said, a Western personality and right-brain dominance presumably explains the Oriental personality). But can the brain do even this unaided? And what of the vast territories, the spiritual world that exists beyond the limits of the brain's frontier and that clearly cannot be experienced by the unregenerate, uninspired, erring mind? Shall we say that these lands that have proven to be so helpful to the inspirational life of mystics do not exist simply because their mysteries cannot be satisfactorily probed by the mind?

The mind of natural man attempts to prove itself *and* rule itself. Many have tried to compromise and to claim for the mind the legal rights to these unchartered and dimly understood lands. Did St. Thomas Aquinas become so entangled? The neo-Thomistic fusion of the Hellenic concept of the "intellectual" with the Judeo-Christian concept of the "spiritual"—the idea that "mind" was equivalent to "spirit"—led to the conclusion that the mind should be allowed to rule the person. This dogma has taken fast hold of man's imagination and has been buttressed by pragmatism, empiricism and scientific materialism. Today, the faintest whisper suggesting that mind may not be the zenith of man's experience leads habitually to the automatic, sceptical retort, "But what else do we have?" In the tussle for mind versus spirit, the mind has abducted the best of man's heritage and claimed the ascendancy.

Currently an altar is being erected to the brain. This altar was previously devoted to the mind. It predated even the apparent decency of the Thomist view; for everywhere, among the heavy clutter of Greek gods and Roman kings, we see the sacrificial smoke weaving from its altars. "Rationalism—all hail its power" was the cry. Today the cry still rises, more articulate than ever before, more daring, more obtrusive. It reasserts itself in the modern religions of the world which offer as man's sole aim, the glory of man.

The altar to the mind has not stood the test. Neither will the altar to the brain.

How does our human pride bedeck itself? The robes of today's human pride are merely hand-me-downs. The age-old cult of rationalism spawned its martyrs, teachers, prophets and leaders on both sides of the Western philosophical fence and has dressed them all in the same time-wearied garb. Whether the children of the Platonic line (Descartes perhaps being the most illustrious) or the sons of Aristotle (Newton, Hume, Comte, Dewey, the extended family of the existentialists being among the most vociferous), all have sung the song in praise of man and his mind to one tune or another. The ditty crops up irrepressibly in the intellectual themes of idealism, positivism, classical realism, pragmatism, behavioural experimentalism and even social reconstructionism. The words found in the rhapsody are selfhood, self-consciousness, self-determination, self-realization, self-integration, self-direction, self-sufficiency or its twin sister self-reliance, self-actualization, self-worth, self-knowledge and unrecognized by most, selfishness. The refrain is independence, autonomy, relativism, democracy and experience. The title is ego, self-centeredness (selfism) and self-will. Most humanists would disclaim this latter statement, arguing that self-actualizing persons are neither self-centered nor selfish. But we must take a hard look at humanism in the light of anthropocentrism. Should the lyrics be subordinated to a responsive love for the Divine, the ditty and its stock concepts will be either rewritten or invested with life. When put on the pedestal where they are most often found, they become dan-gerous, degenerate and often demonic.

One teacher alone in all the world stands apart, majestic, unhurried, unacclaimed by some but unperturbed—not a mere philosopher, good but not just a good man—the Son of God, the Lord Jesus Christ. His claim still resonates in peace and power through the twisted tortures of the world's timeless mime: to find Life, the self must die.

Except a corn of wheat fall into the ground and die, it abideth alone: but if it die, it bringeth forth much fruit... Ye must be born again... (John 12:24, 3:7).

Twentieth-century man refutes the evidence of the centuries. The nineteenth-century hope that reason could be the master of interest and passion and therefore the instrument of increasing universal well-being was erroneous. But the error has been overlooked once again. It is not now generally admitted that reason is always intimately related to self and is more easily the servant than the master of self. Freud knew only too well how skilled the rational mind is in deceiving itself when convenient. His defense mechanisms are testimony to this understanding.

Christ made no compromises; least of all with the self: "*...not my will, but thine...*" (Luke 22:42).

He asks us not for half measures, but for the whole self. He asks us to:

> ...hand over the whole natural self, all the desires which you think innocent as well as the ones you think wicked—the whole outfit. [He promises] I will give you a new self instead. In fact, I will give you Myself: my own Will shall become yours (C.S. Lewis, *The Joyful Christian*).

Christ accepts no compromises.

> Augustine, who was quite great, sufficiently Hellenic, and sufficiently Platonic, did not avoid... a definite conviction that you must impose conversion upon the Greek mind without denying the use of intellect. He would not look for a compromise at this point, he would simply demand conversion... But St. Thomas did compromise (Fuller, *The Christian Idea of Education*).

The compromise referred to earlier, the attempt to fuse the Judeo-Christian with the Hellenistic, to clothe the spiritual with the intellectual, has dulled the spiritual awareness of millions of people and quieted countless questions. To a large extent natural man no longer seeks to discover what exists in the territory beyond the frontiers of the mind. In its senseless hauteur, the mind has quietly hypnotized itself.

Another subgroup of natural man does not seek to eclipse spirit with mind; rather, the error consists in seeking to delimit spirit to man's spirit, leaving no place for the supernatural. Man's spirit in this case is defined as the essence of responsibility, freedom and will.

In natural progression the lust for power in the man of flesh, follows hard on the heels of pride. The exalted self, too high to see another, does not see the Other. The self, the big ego, becomes a god. And gods have rights: the right to look down upon, to survey, to manipulate, to taunt, to torture. If these sad qualities marked the deities of Mount Olympus, how much more the man who sees himself as god! Man as god is never all-giving, beneficent, wise and good and kind. Inevitably, self-interest permeates his best project. He becomes greedy, cruel, ruthless, exploitative, cold. He takes and gives in order to get. He steps on others to achieve his end. It is noticeable that the Messiah is portrayed by Isaiah as a suffering, not as a conquering, Redeemer and that *"...being found in fashion as a man, He humbled Himself and became obedient unto death, even the death of the cross"* (Philippians 2:8).

Power corrupts. It first corrupts the heart of man, then it corrupts his relationship with his brother. It culminates in a socially-corrupt society. For the individual, the big ego that flaunts its flag before the face of the great *I Am*, the end is death, for *"...power belongeth unto God"* (Psalm 62:11).

The mind that sees itself as god is already less than a hairbreadth away from the corrupt heart. It steadily plots and ploys and schemes the evil which proceeds from the heart. The evil of the heart is ominously ugly. The irony is that it customarily makes its entrance dressed in a mask that is alluringly attractive and popularly cute. Its deception is painstakingly slow where necessary but carefully orchestrated. Once inside, it flaunts itself recklessly, revealing all the hideousness of its duplicity and moral decadence. Its destruction is devastating—plain for all to see. But in the beginning this is not so. The devil approaches as an angel of light.

The evil heart that he creates is at first convinced of its purity and its integrity. The clever mind rationalizes the evil intentions of the heart washing them in a sickly counterfeit rinse. Under the spell of this self-beguilement, the heart adjusts itself to unbelief, selfish pleasure, vanity, superiority, envy, greed, hate and fear. Did not Jeremiah, who emphasized inward faith rather than the trappings of religion, observe,

The Growth of the Person

"The heart is deceitful above all things, and desperately wicked: who can know it?" (Jeremiah 17:9).

Power beguiles. It gives man a thirst for superiority. This thirst culminates in the desire to manipulate and to use others, to find a scapegoat. The offender is often not aware of the damage being done.

The lust for power is the seed for hatred which, when it germinates, can rob the doer of caution and restraint; thus Cain, envious, will not be reconciled to his brother but will slay him, without provocation, in the open field.

The virus spreads quickly in the society of fevered brains. We are forced to wonder today whether it is the individual or the society which is afflicted with schizophrenia and its attendant ambivalence. Nettleford, a West Indian scholar trained at Oxford, presents the problem of national schizophrenia. But might it not be global; might it not be more prevalent than is generally thought to be the case?

Man, who aspires to be god and becomes besotted with power, sooner or later begins to worship the devil. In the Western world, the daily news, our literature, our entertainment, our propaganda—all are overbearingly filled with accounts of devil worship, real as well as fictional, of temples to the devil made with man's hands, of human sacrifice, clairvoyancy, extra-sensory perception, mind-reading, necromancy, ouija boards, horoscopes, voodoo, parapsychology and yoga. This is only the beginning of the list. If the fetishes and amulets and children's games incorporating the occult are carefully counted, it is said that they represent an alarming percentage of our economic trade.

In the meantime, the turnover to the consumer occurs at an insidiously rapid rate in the name of availability, fashion and free thought.

To conclude, the homely description of the man of the flesh presents him as ambitious, hardworking, but arrogant, power-loving and thus corrupt.

Paul Tillich, celebrated theologian and philosopher, attempts to solve the dilemma of man's nature by proposing that "Man is basically good and evil."[10] He believes in two kinds of human nature: a "created" nature which is good and a "temporal, historical" nature which is evil. At the risk of being dubbed closed-minded and simplistic, it must be pointed out that in keeping with the Pauline epistle (Galatians 5), goodness and evil are opposed and *"are contrary the one to the other."* They cannot exist in the same breast with any degree of peace. Neither can they operate together. The ethnic cleansing will prevent any pact and will demand that aggression be continued until one or the other is exterminated.

Man Actuated by the Spirit of God

The description of Regenerate Man is definite and precise. It is neither left to our imagination nor to the pen of the speculative. It is firmly rooted in history without the blemish of variation in any epoch. It is based solidly on the Word of God.

Regenerate Man may be described briefly with the aid of the model in Figure 2. An individual is at the entry to the category "Regenerate" when he comes to the turn in the road where he recognizes his condition of sin and his need of a Saviour. There is only one qualification for entry: putting off the old man and putting on the New Man, Christ Jesus.

> *That ye put off... the old man, which is corrupt according to the deceitful lusts... And that ye put on the new man, which after God is created in righteousness and true holiness* (Ephesians 4:22,24).

THE GROWTH OF THE PERSON

> IN RESPECT TO THE THINGS THAT REALLY MATTER,
> WE ARE ALL IN THE SAME BOAT.

I. CREATION = Good

"And God saw everything that he had made, and, behold, it was very good" (Genesis 1:31).

II. FALL = Sin Attitude

"...all have sinned, and come short of the glory of God" (Romans 3:23).

"As by one man sin... even so by the righteousness of one..." (Romans 5:12,18).

Quality = Bad

(Jeremiah 17:9)
(Isaiah 1:3-9)
(1 Samuel. 16:7)

Lust of Flesh
Lust of Eyes
Pride of Life

Differences in degree of natural virtue.

V. REGENERATE COMMITTED = Good

"But of him are ye in Christ Jesus, who of God is made unto us wisdom, and righteousness, and sanctification, and redemption" (1 Corinthians 1:30).

Patience - (2 Peter 1:5-7)
Humility - (Philippians 2)

IV. REGENERATION

Works - Fruit of the Spirit
Faith
Repentance
Responsibility - admit sin

III. SALVATION = One Condition

Colossians 3:10
Ephesians 4:22, 24

Figure 2 - Christian Model: THE NATURE OF MAN

If the individual responsibly admits his sinfulness, repents and exercises faith in the historic work of redemption accomplished by Christ at Calvary, he will benefit from this trust by seeing the fruit of the Spirit in his life (Galatians 5:22). The ultimate aim is that:

> ...*of him are ye in Christ Jesus, who of God is made unto us wisdom, and righteousness, and sanctification, and redemption* (1 Corinthians 1:30).

In this condition and on this condition alone we are restored to the status "good" which was pronounced at the Creation. We regain the status we had before the Fall. But it is the work of the Holy Spirit, not ours, and it is the righteousness of Christ, not ours.

"Regenerate Committed" may be rephrased in so many different ways according to scriptural texts. One of the most beautiful is the gripping passage:

> *But ye are a chosen generation, a royal priesthood, an holy nation, a peculiar people; that ye should shew forth the praises of him who hath called you out of darkness into his marvellous light* (1 Peter 2:9).

The Regenerate condition is not merely a copy nor an imitation of good works but arises from new birth and the new form of relationship to the Creator who has been invited to take the controls. It rests fully on relationship:

> *If a man love me, he will keep my words: and my Father will love him, and we will come unto him, and make our abode with him* (John 14:23).

"Regenerate Committed" means walking in the Spirit and not fulfilling the lusts of the flesh (Galatians 5). There is no other way by which man can be deemed good. The credit for the metamorphosis cannot be given to the creature. It belongs to the Creator all the way. And so it is written, *"nevertheless I live; yet not I, but Christ liveth in me"* (Galations 2:20).

A dispassionate examination of the preceding would seem to indicate that what ought to be discussed is not merely the philosophical question of whether the creature is good or bad but the theological concern of whether, in view of his endangered position, he is rescued or lost.

EVALUATION

Traditionally, psychologists discussing the nature of man have taken one of three positions on a continuum ranging from "bad" to "neutral" to "good." A few like Jung, Erikson, Allport and Rollo May have chosen the middle position. Ewen writes:

> It appears impossible to draw any definitive conclusions about our innate predisposition for good or evil. We may reasonably speculate that Freud's idiosyncratic position at the pessimistic end of the spectrum is overly negative, and that human beings do seem to have at least some innate capacity for (and enjoyment of) constructive growth. But the extreme optimism of a Horney or Rogers also seems unwarranted when we consider the frequency of war, crime and other human evils (Robert Ewen, *Theories of Personality*).

In this respect, the indeterminacy of psychology as a science offers a bleak conclusion.

Fortunately, theology escapes the confusion and offers a point of view which is located on a completely different continuum, *"for man looketh on the outward appearance, but the Lord looketh on the heart"* (1 Samuel 16:7).

Theology is not influenced by the views that enter into philosophical debate. Rather, it is influenced by a unique point of view which is not locked in with the natural and with the ephemeral but with revelation.

Philosophy and psychology are of the earth, earthy and are concerned with the dromedaries and the cataclysms which are met in a survey of history. In its unique position, theology is saying that man, once arrived on this terrestrial sphere, is on probation and on a pilgrimage. He is eternity bound. Turning, therefore, to a source which is admittedly scriptural, we hear Jeremiah, who prophesied between the years 626-587 B.C., saying, *"I the Lord search the heart..."*(Jeremiah 17:10). Jeremiah has to be credited. He cannot be easily brushed aside. He had to deal with a situation which involved captivity and exile. He was not just a novice. He was learned and knew the people with whom he dealt. He knew the genealogies of his day and that they all harkened back to the saga of a serpent which had beguiled Eve and brought about a position whereby man was cursed by the law and bruised by the Fall. True, there are many who profess to be Christian who do not accept Jeremiah's utterance nor others of this ilk, but when it is examined it will be found crucial to our understanding. Faced with this situation, the individual will have to make a decision whether he can say that universal man is bad, good, neutral or benign or whether he must say that man was made good but (has been attacked, has succumbed) is now sick and needs a Physician.

The Christian position sees the certainty of faith in a God who is absolutely good and holy, who made all things good and pronounced them to be so. When He took a second look, man, using his free will, had wrested himself from the caveat in his constitution and had become corrupt and degenerate. In

THE GROWTH OF THE PERSON

His mercy, God provided a way of salvation—the righteousness of His only Son, Jesus Christ: *"...by the righteousness of one the free gift came upon all men unto justification of life"* (Romans 5:18).

> *I will greatly rejoice in the Lord, my soul shall be joyful in my God; for he hath clothed me with the garments of salvation, **he hath covered me with the robe of righteousness**, as a bridegroom decketh himself with ornaments, and as a bride adorneth herself with her jewels* (Isaiah 61:10).

> *Not by works of righteousness which we have done but according to his mercy he saved us...* (Titus 3:5).

> *For if by one man's offence death reigned by one; much more they which receive abundance of grace and of the gift of righteousness shall reign in life by one, Jesus Christ* (Romans 5:17).

The Absolute Truth is very simple, not complicated. There is only one Person who was good. Only the spotless Lamb of God could pay the price for the sins of every human being (Revelation 5:1-14). And so it is written, *"He that hath the Son hath life; and he that hath not the Son of God hath not life"* (1 John 5:12).

PART 2

THE STRUCTURE OF THE PERSON

2. CHOOSING A MODEL:

DISCUSSION

ONE IS ORDINARILY AT A LOSS to know what is the precise nature of the relationship between the brain, its mind and the other components of the human personality referred to in every school of classical thought: the heart, the soul, the spirit, the conscience, the will and the understanding. Would perhaps some of these components act as the gate-keepers to the portals of the mind? Would the function of the conscience, will and the understanding be to monitor the incoming stimuli? Or is it the mind itself which acts as the gaunt sentinel to information seeking to influence the total personality? Where do we really find the controlling factor in human personality?

In our Western society it has at long last become commonly accepted, after what seemed like slow and tortuous diversions by the positivists and the behaviourists, that the physical brain does not stand alone as the sole sentry as it governs the human body but that somewhere within its obscure immaterial environs or in the intimate reaches of its neural operations there is a mind, a selective controlling intelligence. Modern psychology is increasingly more willing to accept the view that human behaviour is not entirely governed by stimuli from the environment which make their way towards the brain via neural receptors, nor can behaviour be entirely predicted from the rewards in the environment associated with previous or imagined response patterns. Psychology has come to the place where it is forced to acknowledge the existence of variables which intervene between the stimulus and the response—the existence, that is, of a personal mind which is perhaps as much dependent on the brain as the brain is dependent on it. Unfortunately, psychology's usual indeterminacy and lack of consensus has also fostered the more recent opinion (see, for example, Richard Restak's *The Brain*) that the physical brain *per se*, with its competencies and deficiencies, is responsible for all the achievements and aberrations of human personality: that the brain has no need of a mind.

At this stage it will be affirmed with no contradiction from any psychological model of learning, that the human being has at least five known portals to the brain. These are the five senses: seeing, hearing, smelling, tasting and feeling. A sixth sense is also acknowledged: the power of intuition. There is a great deal of mystery surrounding this last important facility and yet it has a power which is in no way subordinate to the five. This is a gateway which is certainly more spiritual, less material, more fragile but more pervasive, less logical but certainly influential in the sphere of the will and the determining choice. But is our intuition the final and operative word?

The tentative answers to the preceding questions provide a multiplicity of models—some of which seem to lead to a degree of convergence at any given point, others of which appear to be less conformable to any common pattern perhaps because they are themselves less well structured.

It is the opinion of the author that some of the answers to these questions may be sought, first of all, by an examination of two different dimensions: the structure of the brain and the function(s) of the brain and its mind. Inevitably, the conclusions to the quest must involve an interaction between structure and function. The answers must also rely, in part, on the particular meanings assigned to each of the components of the personality as they may be discerned from a number of philosophies and perspectives.

The existing literature on brain structure and function is already quite divergent. Phrenology (propagated by Gall in the late eighteenth century), with its assumed specific locations and cranial bumps for the development of special faculties (e.g. moral character, intelligence, memory, logical ability, rhetorical skill), has long ago been discarded as a pseudo science. Currently psychology emphasizes at least three distinct models for conceptualizing brain structure depending on the quality and type of brain function hypothesized. First, there is a vast body of literature dedicated to the examination of brain function in terms of the brain's left/right hemispherical structure. The obvious existence of two clearly demarcated lobes connected in the central region by the corpus callosum is, of course, highly suggestive that the functions of the brain are also lateralized. This supposition has led to endless research attempting to support the view that brain functions such as linguistic skills and analytic abilities versus spatial and figurative skills are fairly asymmetrical in the brain and are more directly controlled by one or the other hemisphere (see for example, Gazzaniga, Sperry, Restak). In general, it has been fairly well concluded (save for a few recent rumblings to the contrary) that the left hemisphere of the brain has greater control over analytic, sequential and verbal skills while the right hemisphere is in direct control of spatial skills, intuitive thinking and more global or gestalt-type processing. Elaborate models pertinent to personality theory (e.g. Royce) have been constructed based on the fundamental notion that brain functions are basically lateralized. Even in the area of learning theory and learning styles a plethora of dichotomies related to dominance in left versus right brain functions have been brought forward and presented for application in the educational field. The literature refers unabashedly to presupposed learning styles such as reflexivity versus impulsivity, field dependence versus field independence, narrow versus broad categorizing, and simultaneous versus successive processing among others. These styles each exhibit their strengths in the individual personality depending on the individual's orientation to left or right brain dominance. It appears then that few stones have been left unturned in the attempt to exploit what would seem to be the most extant feature of the brain's physical structure.

The second widely-used model for the discussion of brain structure and function chooses to overlook the apparent dichotomy or lateralization of the brain on the horizontal level and focuses instead on the structure inherent to the vertical dimension as well as the front-to-back dimension (see for example, Das). Briefly, the occipital lobes at the back of the brain are discussed as the prime location of the visual function. Moving forward, the parietal and temporal lobes in the general region above the ears are represented primarily as the central regions for tactile and auditory functions respectively (although it is quickly acknowledged that the complete ramifications of any one function are spread throughout the brain in an intricate interconnection or network of organs which are either essential or ancillary to the function). At the very front of the brain, that is, in the area known as the frontal lobes, higher-order hypothetical functions such as planning are assumed to have their origin. Simultaneous with this front-to-back view of the brain, a vertical structure is considered which is hierarchical in nature. That is, incoming sensory data are processed and stored at the lowest level. At the next higher level this sensory material is organized into concepts as associations are made. At the highest level of brain activity, within the region of the neocortex, both data and their use become increasingly amodal as higher-order integration and conceptualization take place. That is, in the highest regions of the mammalian cortex, thought processes are not dependent on any one single sense.

The third and perhaps most recent model for the examination of brain structure and function centers on the general assumption that the human brain has evolved from that of the lowest vertebrates and this evolution is reflected in its vertical structure. Some hold the view that the human brain is comprised essentially of three separate but intimately interconnected brains, each one representing a different stage in the alleged evolutionary process. The first and lowest, known as the *R-complex*, is similar to the reptilian brain in both structure and function. It covers a network of organs in the brain stem including the medulla oblongata and the pons. McLean has found experimentally that in a variety of species this region of the brain is involved in the preservation of the species and in self-preservation. It governs such functions as hunting, homing, mating, preservation of the territory, fight and flight. Above and around the reptilian brain is the limbic system which humans share with all other mammals. It is otherwise known as the *paleomammalian* brain. It includes organs such as the thalamus, the hypothalamus, the hippocampus and the amygdala. These organs have a wide variety of functions but, taken together, they appear to be directly related to the emotional responses which guide behaviour. McLean claims that after destruction of a part of the limbic system, animals lose their playful and maternal instincts regressing to a reptilian-like condition. The third brain, the cortex or the *neomammalian* brain, is unique to the human species and is responsible for all our higher functions of memory and problem solving. Presumably the human cortex is the control center in this model for specifically human qualities such as symbolic representation, the use of language, reasoning abilities, and the ability to plan for the future and to create a culture.

But is it the brain, or even the mind, which is really in control of human personality? Where do these models lead to outside neurobiology? The diversity of thought experienced in this field is replicated in psychology, philosophy and surprisingly even to a greater degree, theology. Links may be found throughout but they tend to be divergent, loosely connected and sometimes even redundant. Often, when analogous models appear among different fields of thought, they quickly dissipate with the passing of time.

Inspired most likely by the somewhat opposing thought of Plato and Aristotle in the more distant age of classical thought, we find that the contributions of the two greatest medieval theologians, St. Augustine and St. Thomas Aquinas, on the subject of the structure of the personality (the interrelationships between heart, soul, mind, spirit, will, etc.) are already strained by contradictions. In *City of God*, Augustine refers to the soul which governs with its will:

> The virtue which governs a good life controls from the seat of the soul every member of the body, and the body is rendered holy by the act of a holy will.

A few pages further in the same text, we read of the mind as the master of the human being. In addition, this mind may be illumined by a spiritual light. In the ensuing discussion of spirit, Augustine acknowledges that there are two kinds of spirit based on the distinction formed by the Greek words *pneuma* and *pnoé*. In the Greek text of Holy Scripture—the Septuagint—the word *pneuma* is used always to refer to the Holy Spirit of the Trinity. It was also used on the occasion when our Lord breathed on the disciples. But in Genesis 2:7, Scripture declares that *"the Lord God formed man of the dust of the ground, and breathed into his nostrils the breath of life; and man became a living soul."* Here the word *pneuma* is not used but instead the Greek *pnoé*, a word used more frequently for the creature than the Creator and the same word used to apply to animals. Just at the point where Augustine appears to be suggesting that soul is an aspect or type of spirit, however, he declares that these two terms mean the same. For Augustine, emotions are the result of the agreement or disagreement occurring between events in our lives and what we willed regarding these events. The will itself is possessed by the soul. The soul, then, is the active principle in the personality while the body is the passive principle. The spirit is also referred to as the counterpart of the body. One should conclude that for Augustine the soul, mind and the human spirit are all synonymous and that they are to be counterpointed with the body.

Little change could have occurred between the fifth-century writings of St. Augustine and the thirteenth-century writings of the Scholastics as the Church fathers battled with these questions. In the thought of St. Thomas Aquinas, we find much of the same trend towards synthesis occurring.

An attempt to summarize the thinking of Aquinas leads to the conclusion that for him man is a unified nature composed of spirit and matter (body), but spirit is essentially the same as mind and soul in function. The soul cannot be corporeal since it is the first principle of the phenomena and activities of life. As a first principle, it must stand behind all objective corporeal actualities. The noblest acts of the soul are self-movement and knowledge. Defined elsewhere in Aquinas, the soul is the intellectual principle. The substantiality of the soul or intellect inheres in the fact that it performs a function in which the body has no share, although the body does furnish the materials of intellectual knowledge, that is, through its senses. Significant to the thinking of Aquinas is the Aristotelian theory of hylomorphism which states that the principle of intellectual activity, the rational soul, is the essential form of the human body. Matter or body decidedly cannot exist apart from form, but the intellectual life or that which constitutes the first and most basic principle of the activities of a thing is its essential form. The soul, therefore, is the substantial form of the human being. The body is the accidental form superadded to a substance already adequately expressive. As such the soul exists in every part of the body but has special exercise of its powers in the brain. The overlap between "soul" and "mind" is obvious. How does the "spirit" reconcile itself with this redundancy? The answer is that, in the writing of Aquinas, the concept of "spirit" in no way renounces this redundancy but accentuates it. The soul is said to prove its spirituality by virtue of its substantiality. Further, the human soul is indestructible and immortal. Like Augustine, Aquinas holds that our intellect is moved by the light of the divine intellect.

What then are the differences between Aquinas and Augustine? To the eyes of the impartial reader they are perhaps few. It could be said, however, that they are polar and polemic. The controversial issues which disturbed the adherents of Augustine and Aquinas who were viewed as belonging to opposite camps, were not focused directly on the degree of similarity or dissimilarity between soul, mind and spirit, but they were nonetheless fundamental to these questions. The real but important clash between Aquinas (inspired by Aristotle) and Augustine (supported by Plato before him and the Franciscans after him), centered on the question of the source of man's knowledge or the contents of his soul. For the Franciscans and their predecessors, a distinction must be made between our knowledge of the material world which comes to us through the senses and our knowledge of the immaterial world which we acquire through divine inspiration or through the soul's reflection on itself. For Aquinas, all our knowledge starts in the senses and comes to us through experience. If we share in the ideas of the Divine we do so only insofar as the light of our intellect/reason eventually participates in the light of the Divine and is at one with it. There are other differences between the two thinkers.

To emphasize the similarities between Augustine and Aquinas rather than the differences, it would be fair to say that, in keeping with their Greek perspective, they were both persuaded that there was a strong dualism in the human personality and were preoccupied with it. For the Greek, the body (*soma*) is constantly counterpointed with the spirit or mind (*pneuma*) or the vital force which animates the body. Further, the Greek word for flesh (*sarx*), carries the ethical connotation that flesh is evil and corrupts the spirit.

In Greek philosophy, the personality structure was fairly complex. Greek thinking was able to accommodate a basic dualism and at the same time to propose a finely knit overlap among the three components of heart (*kardia*), soul (*psuchee*) and spirit (*pneuma*).

The term heart (*kardia*), both in classical and biblical Greek, means the center of man's personality, thought, affection and volitional desire. In some passages *kardia* refers to either heart, soul or spirit and is used to indicate the seat of the desires, passions, sensations and will. Usually *kardia* refers to the desire cherished with consciousness and expressed with will, reflective volition, resolve and active thought. If a distinction is to be made for the term soul (*psuchee*) at all, it must be found in the idea of the immediate desire which makes its appearance in the form of a natural instinct. Could this be the desire which is unpremeditated and therefore closer to the nature of the body than of the mind? The spirit (*pneuma*) may, like the heart, be possessed of all the qualities of thought, feeling and suffering. We read in the Scriptures of God's love, anger, wrath, hatred of sin, pity, judgment. It must be remembered that the Greek *pneuma* is to be distinguished from the term *pnoé*.

In some strange way then, the three Greek terms heart (*kardia*), soul (*psuchee*), and spirit (*pneuma*) enjoy a peculiar interrelationship and, in one way or another, in the eyes of one thinker or another, all three impinge on both the emotional and rational life.

But is it the heart, though at the center of the personality, which is really in control of the personality? It may be said of the heart that it gets to the bottom of all manifestations of the divine principle of life, be they emotional or rational. In biblical New Testament thought, the activity of the Spirit must be especially sought in the heart. What, in the last instance, belongs to the spirit we can attribute to the heart. In the words of Spiros Zodhiates, we have a beautiful rendition of the centrality of the heart:

> The heart is every man's best part—the shrine of his affections, the ocean of his thoughts, the storehouse of the energies of his will—insomuch that there is not one of the multifarious responsibilities of life which he can worthily bear, nor one of its great duties that he can effectively discharge, until he has learned to put his heart into it. Least of all is it possible for religion to be of value unless it be suffused with the tenderness, glowing with the ardour, and resolute with the purpose of the heart. As we ourselves know that we have never won a man until we have gained his affection, so He who created and redeemed us insists that we have given nothing to Him until we yield our love. Consent of the intellect alone is nothing (*The Commandments of Christ*. An exposition of Matthew 5:8, "Purity").

God is interested in the heart. He is more interested in improving personal relationship with His creature than in any other activity.

The analogy here with the biblical concept of faith is perfect. The characteristic construction for "saving faith" is that wherein the verb *pisteuo* is followed by the preposition *eis*. Literally, this means to believe "into." It denotes a faith which, so to speak, takes a man out of himself and puts him into Christ (cf. the expression frequently used of Christians being "in Christ"). This faith is not just a belief that carries an intellectual assent, but is one in which the believer cleaves to his

Saviour with all his heart. It is an abiding in Christ. Faith is not accepting certain things as true, but trusting a person, and that Person is Christ.

Hebrew psychology and theology contain none of the dualism commonly found in Greek writing and impregnated into New Testament thought. The Hebrew has no word for body in the same sense that the Greek *soma* is used. The word used to refer to created man, man the creature, is *basar* (Genesis 6:17) and is usually translated "flesh." It is used to refer likewise to all living creatures and carries none of the connotation of corruption attributed to the flesh by St. Paul in the New Testament. In spite of this absence of dualism in Hebrew thinking, the Hebrew personality is endowed with just as intricate and finely synthesized a structure as that of the Greek. The personality is characterized by its wholeness and unity, however, to an extent that is even greater than that found in Greek thinking.

To elucidate, in examining the components of the personality as expressed in Hebrew thought we find some of the same overlaps and redundancies found in Greek thinking but with significant modifications, some minor and some major.

The body or flesh, *basar*, not being endowed with the vilification and corruption which marks the Greek word *sarx* used by Paul to denote carnality, is easily integrated into the higher levels of the personality to effect the wholeness and unity anticipated. Flesh in *basar* does not imply moral defect as it does in the Pauline epistles with the use of *sarx*, therefore, man can accept his creatureliness without fear of any corrupting influence. There is no danger of an ascetic rejection of the body as evil! (Properly understood, this is also true of the New Testament Greek *soma* [body] which, in the regenerate person, is "a temple of the Holy Spirit."[11] The Hebrew, however, does not hesitate to acknowledge the limitations and the powerlessness of the *basar*. Throughout the Old Testament, the weakness of the creaturely man as opposed to the power of God is brought out. The people of God are told not to trust in the "arm of flesh."

Power then becomes the overriding characteristic of the Hebrew concept of spirit (*ruach*). It is God who has the power to move man. The Hebrew does not put his faith in flesh but in God. Whether the term *ruach* is translated power or breath or wind or spirit, all indications are that it is something which comes from God. It is that which makes the clod of dust into a living person. This power is both teleological and creative. It is this power which makes for wholeness of the person. *Ruach* is the principle of life itself and is comparable to the Greek term *pneuma*.

Whitlock (1983),[12] from his in-depth interpretation of the Old Testament, provides one explanation of the Hebrew structure of personality. He arrives at four distinct meanings for the Hebrew *ruach*. First, as the vital principle of life, it develops into that which means the unseen element in man which expresses itself in the spirit of man or in his rational mind and senses, affections and emotions. Rahab told the spies from Joshua, *"And as soon as we heard these things, our hearts did melt, neither did there remain any more courage* (ruach) *in any man…"* (Joshua 2:11). This courage is from God. Thus it is courage or the "courage to be" (Tillich) which quickens man and prevents him from being a mere clod of earth. Secondly, *ruach* is used to indicate will or counsel. As will, it refers to the self-assertion of the person (1 Chronicles 5:26). As counsel, it refers to that which arises in the mind or occupies the mind (1 Chronicles 28:11-12). Third, *ruach* is used as spirit in the sense that it is applied to the intellect or understanding. Fourth, the term indicates a mode of thinking and acting. Since *ruach* in the Old Testament does not refer to the essence of God but to His power, it is not to be understood as a faculty given to man but is to be understood in a functional sense. When the various concepts of *ruach* are used they appear in action. *Ruach* describes the functioning of the total organism through courage and self-control. It is expressed in the total organism—in the emotions, the intellect, the will but above all in the actions. Man has the responsibility to act, but it is the *Ruach* of God which gives him the power to act.

The *nephesh* (soul) is the component of the personality which creates the bridge between the *basar* (flesh) and the *ruach* (spirit). It is the vital principle of life itself caused by the fusion of the *basar* and the *ruach* as in the creation story (Genesis 2:7), and without which the person dies (1 Kings 17:21). It is, for the most part, a reference to the concrete individual and is that which bears the individual personality. The *ruach* is the power which moves the individual but it is the *nephesh* which exhibits the power or energy. It refers to the total life of man including both biological and psychic life—that is, it indicates a concept of organismic unity. The Hebrew believed that man was essentially a unity. In its all-encompassing meaning, *nephesh* is often used to refer to the mind as the seat of the senses, affections and emotions. It is even used to refer to the experience of love (Genesis 34:3). Above all, however, the *nephesh* presents the organism as a unitary whole without any of the dualisms and dichotomies of the Greeks who maintained a strict distinction between mind and matter.

Whitlock concludes that the presentation of the *nephesh* as the human person in his/her totality has definite implications for theology. In Hebrew thinking it is the total "I" who confronts God. Man is responsible for bringing his total self into involvement. Neither wholeness nor holiness will be secured if the self remains segmented and either the *soma* or the *psyche* is withdrawn from involvement in the confrontation. Further, neither wholeness nor holiness will be achieved through man's own efforts; the flesh (*basar*) is powerless to act. It is the Spirit (*Ruach*) of God which enables man to become a whole person (*nephesh*). *"It is the spirit that quickeneth; the flesh profiteth nothing"* (John 6:63).

Modern theological interpretations of the nature of the person are, of course, not restricted to Whitlock's work. Among numerous other commentators, the views of Beechick and Arendt are of particular interest.

Beechick (1982),[13] has categorized references to the heart in the Bible under at least six headings. The heart refers first to the material organ although references of this type are scanty. Second, it speaks of the spiritual life of understanding and belief in the parable of the sower (Matthew 13:19); of unbelief (Hebrews 3:12); of the indwelling of the Spirit (2 Corinthians 1:22); of the peace of God (Colossians 3:15); of the love of God (Romans 5:5). The Scripture which caps them all in the opinion of the author is 2 Corinthians 4:6:

> *For God, who commanded the light to shine out of darkness, hath shined in our hearts, to give the light of the knowledge of the glory of God in the face of Jesus Christ.*

Third, Beechick sees the term heart being used to refer to the moral life. There are Scriptures dealing with the heart as the tablet on which the work of the law is written (Romans 2:5); with the discriminating power of the heart in knowing what is good and what is evil and as acting as the seat of the conscience (Hebrews 10:22); with the heart as loving God or being lifted up in pride against Him (Ezekiel 28:2,5).

Fourth, there are numerous Scriptures dealing with the heart as the seat of the emotions. In this respect it is clear that emotions are in God's heart too (Hosea 11:8). Fifth, the heart is the well-acknowledged source of the motivations whereby one wills to do good or evil (Daniel 1:8, Ecclesiastes 8:11). The sixth and final category refers to the use of the heart to describe the thought life. The heart not only knows things but considers, ponders and meditates upon them (Luke 2:19, Psalm 19:14).

Hanna Arendt, in her work *The Life of the Mind*, makes an unusual distinction for a Jewess, between the soul and the mind. Yet it seems to have the potential to be quite suggestive. Everywhere else in the literature, even in Hebrew psychology where the soul comes nearest to being identified with the body or the flesh, the term "soul" retains some degree of connection with the life of the mind and the thoughts. However, Arendt sees fit to sever the connection between soul and mind. Her striking contribution is to pronounce that evil can be construed as the absence of thought. In saying this, evil seems to be assigned to the soul, the seat of the emotions, passions and moods. The display of emotions seen in the face and other expressive movements of the body constitute the work of the soul, says Arendt. Ordinarily, man needs considerable training in self-control to prevent self-display (that is, the unchecked demonstration of his emotions) and to offer instead self-presentation (that is, the selective presentation of those emotions which he wishes to be seen). A mindless creature, says Arendt, is at the mercy of its inner life processes, its moods, its emotions... If this is true, the present writer agrees that the work of the soul may properly be represented as the gage of the existence of evil. Arendt is right insofar as Scripture requires the practice of self-control referred to as temperance. Scripture teaches, however, that we need more than just controlled self-presentation, that is, a display of emotions controlled by the mind. We need cleansing.

The preceding views on the structure of the person, whether they are based on classic theological opinion or on more recent thought, all indicate that the brain and/or its mind are inextricably implicated in the working of the total person, whether attention is focused on the heart, the soul, the spirit or the will. Although in these writings the emotional is sometimes separated from the rational in very incidental and subordinate ways, in all major definitions they function together. Scientific probing into the brain's functions has already confirmed the fact that emotional processes are just as much related to brain activity as rational processes are.

The theological implication of this for man's relationship with God is that the brain and the mind are irrevocably involved in the total process whether one is referring to the intimate and secret desires of the heart and its conscious strivings or to the more objective and rational life of the intellect. To elaborate further, there has been an erroneous and detrimental tendency over the centuries to equate the heart and the mind with the emotional and the rational, respectively, and to ignore the basic need that each has for the other and the intricate interaction between the two. This confusion has led to unnecessarily distinct schools of thought: the one protagonist holding that we are called to love with all our heart and thus with an emphasis on the emotional, the other protagonist asserting that since spirit is, in scholastic thought, synonymous with mind our prime service to God is to give Him our rational intellect. If these confusions are real, and they appear to be so, then it is unfortunate. Theological and religious circles need to agree, at least, on the essential and necessary integration of man as a servant of God.

The apparent overlap existing between the heart and the mind is expressed nowhere more clearly than in the Bible itself. There it is plain that the heart, traditionally held as the seat of the emotions, is the center of the intellectual and volitional life of man (Romans 10:9-10), that the heart has thoughts and that these thoughts fall within the purview of consciousness (Matthew 9:4, 15:9; Mark 7:21,22; Luke 2:19, 2:51, 5:22, 9:47, 24:38; Acts 8:21,22). Fleck and Carter,[14] make the point that although inner thoughts occur within the field of consciousness, a person may not observe or notice them. By shifting his attention, however, he can become more aware of them and can delineate their content.

Indications of the essential fusion of spirit, mind, heart and soul in the Bible are unending. There we are told, *"Set your affection on things above, not on things on the earth"* (Colossians 3:2). "Set your affection on," which is the translation of *phroneo*, is a paraphrase of the literal meaning "to think" or "to set the mind on." Then again we are told to be *"renewed in the spirit of your mind"* (Ephesians 4:22-25). In Ephesians 2:3-6 we are reminded that the mind can be carnal and that it is just as subject to lust as is the flesh. Earlier, in Proverbs 23:7, we are told that *"as a man thinketh in his heart so is he,"* and in Matthew 15:18,19 the Lord Himself pronounces that *"out of the heart proceed evil thoughts."*

EVALUATION

It should be clear that the presentation developed in this chapter acknowledges the cooperation of the brain and the mind with every other aspect of the person, whether it be the heart, the soul or the spirit. But the interpretations of the term mind itself are to be taken with loose connotations often invading even the territory of the heart in scriptural language. A caution which has hitherto been inserted only implicitly will now be elaborated. The popular notion exists, not really supported by Scripture, that since the mind is the most highly developed aspect of the human race there really is no better agent of the human totality to be in control! In the light of the foregoing this is, of course, incorrect. What needs to be made clear is that reason *per se* (based on defense mechanisms, excuses and rationalizations) is precisely what we use in our own self defeat. The only true antidote for sin is the scriptural one, *"Walk in the spirit and ye shall not fulfill the lust of the flesh"* (cf. the lusts of the mind are to be included) (Galatians 5:16). The individual needs to understand that it is the inflowing Spirit of God which quickeneth; the flesh, that is, the *sarx* (which may include the rationalizations of the mind in the New Testament Greek rendition), "profiteth nothing."

A complement to this last point may be found in Hebrew psychology and theology. Since it is the *ruach* of God that enables the committed believer to act in any way whatsoever, it is the Spirit of God who enables the individual to become a whole person in relatedness with other persons in community. It is the Spirit of God who empowers man to turn from his natural egocentricity and to develop a God-consciousness rather than a self-consciousness.

Kierkegaard, in *The Sickness Unto Death*, outlines an ontology which elevates the spirit of man above the soul (mind). For him, spirit is the absolute of all that a man can be. In his existential psychology, man's chief dilemma is to become a self or spirit. To this end he must experience a certain kind of anxiety which for Kierkegaard is good. This is the anxiety which stirs and motivates a man to arise, answer the call and the challenge and become the best that he can be. This anxiety points to the "creative directive to become oneself in truth, relentlessly," and is therefore God-given.

Instead of focusing on anxiety in the search for spirit and assigning the priority to this, the present author prefers the scriptural injunction which speaks of knowing the *"love of Christ which passeth knowledge"* (Ephesians 3:19). This is the motivating power of the Spirit which synthesizes the other components of body, heart, soul and mind.

The battle of attempting to understand the fine shades of personality structure continues in numerous schools of thought. In attempting to answer the question "what or who controls the personality," the author wishes to end the debate by quoting the words of C.S. Lewis in *The Joyful Christian*:

> Christ says "Give me all. I don't want so much of your time and so much of your money and so much of your work: I want you. I have not come to torment your natural self, but to kill it. No half-measures are any good. I don't want to cut off a branch here and a branch there, I want to have the whole tree down. I don't want to drill the tooth, or crown it, or stop it, but to have it out. Hand over the whole natural self, all the desires which you think innocent as well as the ones you think wicked—the whole outfit. I will give you a new self instead. In fact, I will give you Myself: my own Will shall become yours."

3. THE HEALTHY PERSON:

MENS SANA IN CORPORE SANO?

> Reason's last step is the recognition that there are an infinite number of things which are beyond it. It is merely feeble if it does not go as far as to realize that.
>
> Pascal, *Pensées*

PSYCHOLOGY HAS BEEN DEEPLY imbued with the belief that the mind is at the helm of the human personality. There are even those who have abdicated ownership or responsibility for all of our qualities, aptitudes and characteristics and handed them to the brain and its chemical processes. Say to a modern scientist that the brain is the most sophisticated computer and he is likely to agree. Up to a point the modern scientist is correct.

The brain and the mind, like the computer, are brilliant masterpieces. Based on their accumulated knowledge, they both evidence a certain degree of versatility, productivity and insight which would normally escape the passing dilettante, and sometimes a characteristic which may even be called creativity. But they are all three incorrigibly neutral. As the scientist well knows, "one takes out of the computer only what one has put in!" The brain and the mind, invaluable as they are, are totally dependent on the operator. The brain does not drive itself, it is driven. What is fed into it is what comes out. Consequently the same brain may be stimulated by the loftiest thoughts or actuated or impelled by the most ignoble. It depends entirely on the character of the operator chosen to be in command, on the openness of the mind to the dimension of the spirit and on what the ancients called inspiration or the inflowing breath of God. The brain, as a vehicle of the spirit and the mind, is only a neurological instrument.

Where is this life of the Spirit to be found? Is it inherited by the accident of natural birth, by the fact of status, by the accomplishment of good works and deeds? No. The Nazarene Himself, He whom all true Christians must follow, made it abundantly clear. He Himself said, *"That which is born of the flesh is flesh; and that which is born of the Spirit is spirit"* (John 3:6). It begins when a man sees himself for what he really is—fallen, poor, wretched, needy, and goes to the foot of the cross.

What does he do there? He acknowledges his sins, for, *"...all have sinned and come short of the glory of God"* (Romans 3:23). He accepts the eternal gift of God's Son, the Lamb sacrificed in his place for his sin and pleads the blood of the Lamb as a covering for his sins. *"Blessed is he whose transgression is forgiven, whose sin is covered"* (Psalm 32:1). For the Lord is *"...of purer eyes than to behold evil, and canst not look on iniquity"* (Habakkuk 1:13). He decides, with every fibre of his will—God being his helper—to cease from practising sin. He loses his guilt and knows the ecstasy of this loss. Only then can he truly begin to communicate with God. For many, this is a hard thing to do. It requires humility. The controls must pass from the Adamic spirit and man must admit that he is totally dependent on God for his salvation. It is difficult, but if we recognize our inability to be humble, and seek help, God Himself will help us.

What is this life of the Spirit? It is neither transcendentalism nor spiritualism nor the rhapsodies of human "peak experiences." It is a new life lived on the level of the supernatural. It is not just an experience, but a relationship. It is a relationship with the most real living Person. Let those who wish to espouse the claims of contemporary leaders in other faiths do so. But the writer, like millions of other believers, can recommend to those who are seeking the way, the offices of the Lord Jesus Christ.

> *...if any man hear my voice, and open the door, I will come in to him, and will sup with him, and he with me* (Revelation 3:20).

What is the nature of this relationship? Let it be understood that this relationship is better experienced than told and there is no human pen which can describe and no earthly language which can depict adequately the metamorphosis "unless to mortal it were given to dip his brush in dyes of heaven" (Sir Walter Scott, *Marmion*). This relationship is not a dictatorship. The Lord Himself was opposed to any form of legalism, mass treatment or oppression. He relates to each person in terms of their particular need. It is not democracy, as high as this claim can be. It is theocrasy.

On our part, the relationship is one of love:

> *We love him, because he first loved us* (1 John 4:19);

of adoration:

> *For it pleased the Father that in him should all fulness dwell* (Colossians 1:19);

of worship:

> *...true worshippers shall worship the Father in spirit and in truth* (John 4:23);

of willing obedience:

> *Behold, to obey is better than sacrifice* (1 Samuel 15:22);

of peace:

> *And the peace of God, which passeth all understanding, shall keep your hearts and minds through Christ Jesus* (Philippians 4:7).

On the part of the Lord Jesus, the relationship is one of the lover:

> *O Jerusalem, Jerusalem, thou that killest the prophets, and stonest them which are sent unto thee, how oft would I have gathered thy children together, even as a hen gathereth her chickens under her wings, and ye would not* (Matthew 23:37);

of intimate communion as each believer explores for himself the Word of God:

> *...the words that I speak unto you, they are spirit, and they are life* (John 6:63).

Christ lives in the Word and makes Himself accessible through the Word for He *is* the Word incarnate.

THE GROWTH OF THE PERSON

And the Word was made flesh, and dwelt among us, (and we beheld his glory, the glory as of the only begotten of the Father,) full of grace and truth (John 1:14).

Further, in this relationship the Lord Jesus imparts to us His Holy Spirit to be our helper, the Paraclete, the One who comes alongside us and walks with us. It is here the life of the Spirit assumes its most glorious perfection and its sweetest pleasure. While it befits us, with every ounce of strength, to worship and adore the Lord Jesus in gratitude, the Holy Spirit Himself blesses this sincere worship and transforms it from the rigour of its earthly oughtness to the blissful incense which delights the heart of God and, at the same time, bathes the worshipper in the glory of God. The believer is raised to new heights of unspeakable joy in the Holy Ghost and Christ is experienced in the splendour of His glory.

As our Paraclete, the Holy Spirit illuminates and quickens the soul, He cleanses the heart of its carnal nature, its grossness, its peevishness, its folly. *"It is the spirit that quickeneth; the flesh profiteth nothing"* (John 6:63). *"And you hath he quickened, who were dead in trespasses and sins"* (Ephesians 2:1).

The ministry of the Person of the Holy Spirit is multi-faceted. He raises us to new Life (Romans 8:11), He renews the mind (Ephesians 4:23), He helps our infirmities (Romans 8:26), He teaches us (John 16:13), He searches our hearts (Psalm 51), He intercedes for us in prayer (Romans 8:26), He leads us in battle (Matthew 4:1; Ephesians 6:17), He rejoices over us (Zephaniah 3:17), He heals our memories and helps us to forgive (Luke 4:18,19), He creates in our lives the priceless fruit of His presence—the love, the joy, the peace and the wisdom that surpass human understanding (Galatians 5:22). He comforts us but does not make us complacent. Rather, He troubles us to action and challenges our conceit. While He will "bend over backwards" not to violate our wills, the beautiful and paradoxical mystery of the Holy Spirit is that God Himself worketh in us *"both to will and to do of his good pleasure"* (Philippians 2:13). He makes us more intrusive where this is necessary but He also gives us limits to our interventions so that we do not offend. Above all, He helps us to see Jesus.

Notwithstanding the fact that man is a creature of time and that a metamorphosis must occur on different levels to enable him to experience the reconstruction required for passage into eternity, it can be said that the heart is so made that man is able to pick up the voice of his Master. We do not pretend to know how this occurs but we know it is done.

What, if anything, does the life of the Spirit have to do with reason? Is it possible that reason and faith are complementary, compatible, or must one be jettisoned in favour of the other?

Several extremist views have been advanced, elaborated and exchanged over the centuries. On the one hand, the old Platonic view that the ideal man was the man of reason; that his powers of rational thought were so finely tuned that the gross discords of the appetites, passions and the senses were completely dominated by its harmony; that such a man could not distinctly hear the promptings of the heart for his emotions and even his will were submissive to his reason and, normally, he did a thing because he believed it to be good; that reason was the royal road to salvation. This view has outlived the climatic changes of the centuries. When challenged by its opponents, among them the orthodox religions of the Middle Ages, the view was once again reinforced and ratified in the thirteenth century by St. Thomas Aquinas who placed reason on an equal footing with the life of the Spirit and publicly proclaimed that the intellect was, in essence, spiritual. Today, reason has been divested of the spiritual garb in which it had been rashly wrapped, but it remains snobbish and secure at the vanguard of all those ideologies that recklessly advocate rationalism, self-determinism and free thought.

On the other hand, we see the banner for faith carried unfailingly by a line of zealots as old as the other army who proudly sing the battle cry for reason. Many of the adherents to the cause of faith were churchmen who placed their claims on the Word of God but who, at times, were excessive and caustic in their repeal of reason. A classic example of scepticism towards reason is to be found in Pascal's *Pensées*. This correct yet, in a sense, severe attitude on the part of churchmen made it possible for reason to be identified as "the devil's bride." But must reason in effect be put aside by faith and given a vacation? Is there no way in which reason and faith may be reconciled? Indeed, they must be.

On the level of the abstract, where reason is pure thought (notably logical thought) and faith is pure hope, there is no chance of intermarriage nor even of acquaintance between the two. What is logical can easily be wrong. This has been admitted by the best of minds and tested empirically time and again. This continues every day to be one of science's latest discoveries. Contrary to logical reason, faith—as conviction and as the "evidence of things not seen"—by its very nature does not admit the possibility of error. It is therefore incompatible with reason. Heidegger recognized this in his essays when he said:

> Faith is so absolutely the mortal enemy that philosophy does not even begin to want in any way to do battle with it… Accordingly, there is no such thing as a Christian philosophy; that is an absolute "square circle" (*The Piety of Thinking*).

On the level of action, however, where Christianity rightly belongs, the dichotomies begin to fade. Immediately, we are forced to look more closely to see which virtue, reason or faith, merits the dominant role.

We are told, uncompromisingly, in the Scriptures that we are saved by grace, through faith. This faith is not only an initial faith but a daily, moment-by-moment, ongoing faith which must resist principalities and powers and temptations and which must overcome challenges. It does not give place to reason. It is primary, preeminent and unapologetic. It is ambitious and committed. The eminence of faith in the walk of the Christian is unquestionable. It is by faith that Christ lives in our hearts (Ephesians 3:17). We are justified by faith and not by works (Galatians 2:16) and made righteous by faith (Romans 10:1-14). To intensify further the criterion of faith, we find that the Holy Spirit is received by faith (Galatians 3:2). We cannot pray without faith (James 1:6), have peace with God without faith (Romans 5:1) nor experience joy without faith (1 Peter 1:8). Ultimately, whatsoever is not of faith is sin. Faith is the moving, achieving power in the life of the Christian. It was by faith that the disciples answered the call on a daily basis and left their boats to mingle with the seashore crowds.

Yet faith in action needs reason in action. The reference to reason here is not to pure logic. Once again, this has been tried, judged and sentenced as inadequate, unfit, even ironically, at times, familiar with the flagrantly erroneous. In modern times, contrary to the thinking of the Enlightenment, we have learned that often man uses his logical reason to justify what he desires. This was also admitted by Spinoza:

> We neither strive for, wish, seek, nor desire anything because we judge that it is good, but on the contrary, we judge something to be good because we strive for it, wish it, seek it, and desire it (*Ethics*, iii 9).

THE GROWTH OF THE PERSON

This is eminently so when the thing desired relates to man's passions. The Scriptures concur here and speak of the *"lusts of the flesh, fulfilling the desires of the flesh and of the mind"* (Ephesians 2:3). There seems to be little point in placing one's decisions under the rule of logical reason. Here they are not likely to be any more secure than when left under the sway of volatile emotions.

What then is "reason in action"? It is incipient will. Reason in action can only help if it can be turned over to the Spirit who sublimates it and knits it with faith. Spirit is the repository of faith. When this occurs, the individual experiences strength of character, control, the power to choose the right at the time that the choice is made, the power to carry out the promise, the commitment, the wish, the power to apply past insights, perceptions and precious learnings at the appropriate time. Reason in action must be subjected to faith not to logical thought, for faith alone is unswerving, unfickle, relentless, constant in intent and free of "defense mechanisms." Reason in action is a crucial instrument of faith. The meeting of reason in action and faith, in the Spirit, is illustrated by the apostle Paul when he says, *"Stand therefore..."* (Ephesians 6:13,14), or, in another instance, *"Have faith in God"* (Mark 11:22) because there are grounds for so doing.

The existential, momentary necessity for will is indispensable although secondary to faith. Its role is befittingly described by Fuller:

> God is the Teacher; and part of His purpose is that we shall learn that manhood has got to be chosen, that it is not simply the sum of the things that happen to us or the things we buy but it is a story which we write by our own choice (*The Christian Idea of Education*).

When reason in action is properly controlled by faith, and when the power to will keeps its eyes on the Goal, we avoid becoming the despotic horror or the cruel psychopath or even the fiendish failure. This is where true human virtue begins.

It should not be concluded, however, that reason in action is the sole servant of faith. Abstract formal thought, though not essential, is an advantage. The true man of faith is not a mindless, unthinking, unresourceful creature void of abstract formal thought. He continues, as an integrated person, to think on the abstract level. There, though he is certainly not left to the mercy of the deceits of logical thought, he continues in creative purposeful thinking which is regenerated, quickened, renewed by the Holy Spirit. This is where true human virtue continues.

> *That ye put off concerning the former conversation the old man... And be renewed in the spirit of your mind* (Ephesians 4:22,23).

The practice of sane thinking (*mens sana*) is not far from the concept of faith nor alien to Christianity. Moreover, it is intertwined with every scriptural exhortation, counsel and dogma. The Christian is encouraged to apply right thinking as he reviews his past life, involves himself in the present and looks towards the future. In right thinking he reminds himself that there is "no condemnation" for past mistakes that are forgiven, that there is the Heavenly Paraclete (He who comes alongside to help) for present problems, that there is a glorious hope for the future in Christ's return. This is all synthesized in the injunction given in Philippians 4 and intended to permeate every aspect of our thinking:

> *...whatsoever things are true, whatsoever things are honest, whatsoever things are just, whatsoever things are pure, whatsoever things are lovely... think on these things* (Philippians 4:8).

THE GROWTH OF THE PERSON

The saga of Christian faith therefore, is irrevocably and judiciously mixed with that of human reason. In the human realm strength is never born of schism but of synthesis. In fact, it may be recalled that the truly spiritual man is the one whose entire experience is infused with the power of the Holy Spirit—who loves the Lord his God with all his heart (the deepest desires, emotions, attitudes), all his soul, all his mind and all his strength.

Science has related the physical phenomena of the human person to the content and mechanisms of the brain; physical phenomena such as our size, weight, strength, life expectancy, our ability for gross and fine coordination in motor movement, our receptivity and interpretation of sensory stimuli from the environment, our acuity in establishing spatial relations with the environment—all these skills and qualities are known to have their roots in the brain. Someday, the workings of the brain may be scientifically demonstrated to have more than passing influence in the areas of the mind and soul, the emotions, and to be intimately involved with the will. Already we have seen that skills related to ability for speech, music, drawing, pattern perception, imagination, creativity, affectivity of response, among others, appear to be related to brain structure and function in fairly consistent and possibly predictable ways. That is, theory and research on brain lateralization (left versus right hemispheric structure and function) have attempted to relate specific mental functions and skills to the different hemispheres of the brain and have seemingly contributed small ions to our understanding of the "whole man." Thus, while the mystery of the brain and the mind still evades us, it promises to come within our reach.

However, the study of the physical human brain and even the natural mind will never lead us to a complete understanding of the life of the Spirit. For this, we must open ourselves to the transforming power of the Person of the Holy Spirit Himself. It is He who lifts us to the realm of faith, who helps us to share in the love of God, who teaches us the value of the will of God as against the will of man, who changes the deep attitudes, motives and desires of the inner man, who quickens to us the words of Christ, and ultimately, who allows us to transcend the realm of reason, logic and intellectual belief in order to move mountains, to pass through the gates of eternal life and find company with Jesus, here and now. In all of this, the brain and its mind (rational and emotional) are but the raw materials with which the Spirit works.

Where the Spirit is there is no fear, only peace. When the shutters are flung open wide and the light is welcomed in, every dark corner is permeated, purged, polished. There is no more darkness. The darkness cannot extinguish the light. There is no longer confusion, hatred, intolerance, false imagining, misinterpretation; there is no more anxiety, anger, alarm; no distortions, contortions, clamourings; no depressions, repressions, hauteur, condemnation; no false accusations, manipulations, exploitations; no envy; no greed; no lust; no riotous living; no self-righteousness. There is peace and love.

Pure emotions do not dissipate. Nor does virtuous thought. Human thought, defective and defunct, must be washed, combed and secured by the Holy Spirit into the beautiful, delicate tapestry of faith, resulting in the experience referred to by C.S. Lewis in *Surprised by Joy*:

> As the dry bones shook and came together in that dreadful valley of Ezekiel's, so now a philosophical theorem, cerebrally entertained, began to stir and heave and throw off its graveclothes, and stood upright and became a living presence. I was to be allowed to play at philosophy no longer.

4. THE SPECIAL PEOPLE

But ye are a chosen generation, a royal priesthood, an holy nation, a peculiar people; that ye should shew forth the praises of him who hath called you out of darkness into his marvelous light (1 Peter 2:9).

THE INDIVIDUAL WHOSE HEART is being purified is a prime candidate for becoming a special person. He cannot remain on the threshold indefinitely. He must make a decision. No vacillations are allowed. To enter the realm of holiness we are called to serve not as a double-minded man who prays insincerely but to serve with singleness of mind. No deviations are tolerated. He cannot run with the hare and hunt with the hounds. There is no provision for playing on both sides. We cannot serve two masters, for either we will *"hate the one and love the other"* or we will *"hold to the one, and despise the other"* (Matthew 6:24). To tread the path of the royal priest, we must, in the way of the example given to us, be cleansed of pettiness, petulance and permissiveness. The hallmark of the special person is the heart whose rational and emotional functions have been fused into a unity of expression, direction and purpose and sealed by the will of the Spirit.

The expression "the Special People" anticipates a people who have yielded the self to the will of God. Lest this appear to deny the human being his right to selfhood and autonomy, it must be clarified. It is not the self-effacing servility of the subdued slave. Nor is this submission the gracelessness of the spineless drifter whose sense of will is deflated. Rather, it is the power and poise of the lieutenant who personally knows the Commander-in-Chief.

Paul Tillich has this to say:

> Autonomy does not mean the freedom of the individual to be a law to himself.... Autonomy means the obedience of the individual to the law of reason, which he finds in himself as a rational being. The *nomos* (law) of *autos* (self) is not the law of one's personality structure. It is the law of subjective-objective reason; it is the law implied in the logos structure of mind and reality. Autonomous reason, in affirming itself in its different functions and their structural demands, uses or rejects that which is merely an expression of an individual's situation within him and around him. It resists the danger of being conditioned by the situation of self and world in existence. It considers these conditions as the material which reason has to grasp and to shape according to its structural laws.

Therefore, autonomous reason tries to keep itself free from "ungrasped impressions" and "unshaped strivings." Its independence is the opposite of wilfulness; it is obedience to its own essential structure, the law of reason which is the law of nature within mind and reality, and which is divine law, rooted in the ground of being itself (*Systematic Theology*).

But true autonomy has to be more than mere reason. While obedience to and faith in divine will are never irrational, they may be suprarational. Nor is this dangerous to the existence of the self as some may suppose, for:

> The self can only be exhumed from an egocentric burial ground by hitching itself to something outside itself. It is not germane to its nature to be preoccupied with itself. It has to be committed to something... that will draw it out (Finch, in H.N.Maloney, *A Christian Existentialist Psychology*).

Thus we find the paradoxical mystery that the motivating force in the charismatic personality of the Christ was that He purposed to sacrifice everything in Himself that would detract from the vision of the Father as the final Authority. For this reason, on one memorable occasion, He set His face steadfastly to go to Jerusalem. His desire was not to be a leader, a reformer, a revolutionary, an orthodox Jew, nor even a model son. The one desire which could transform the compassion in His face into the resistant, steely strength of flint, was His will to carry the will of the Father through to completion.

A "peculiar people" cannot be a people of fear. This is so because one's fear object is one's faith object. It is for this reason that the twelve Hebrew spies were so severely reprimanded and punished by God when they were sent to make reconnaissance in preparation for taking the land of Canaan. Their reply—*"we were in our own sight as grasshoppers, and so we were in their sight"* (Numbers 13:33)—was tantamount to idolatry (Morosco, in Maloney). With the exception of Joshua and Caleb, all surrendered to the authority of the Canaanites. The awe and respect due to God as the highest authority had been supplanted.

Since the biblical counterpart of fear is not merely hope, but love, a "peculiar people" must bear the mark of love. Tillich understood the supremacy and the exceptionality of love when he argued:

> No situation which Jesus faced and no act through which he met it establishes an absolutism of dogmatic or moral character... There is, however, an absolute law which can stand under the criterion of finality because it is not denied in the act of self-sacrifice but rather fulfilled. The law of Love is the ultimate law because it is the negation of law; it is absolute because it concerns everything concrete. The paradox of final revelation, overcoming the conflict between absolutism and relativism, is love... Love is always love; that is its static and absolute side. But love is always dependent on that which is loved, and therefore it is unable to force final elements on finite existence in the name of an assumed absolute. The absoluteness of love is its power to go into the concrete situation, to discover what is demanded by the predicament of the concrete to which it turns. Therefore, love can never become fanatical in a fight for an absolute, or cynical under the impact of the relative (*Systematic Theology*).

The peculiar (special) people are very much wanted in today's world. Their peculiarity does not arise from a withdrawal syndrome. While they are called upon to separate themselves from worldliness, they are expected to identify themselves with the various movements in the areas of reconstruction and spiritual rehabilitation. Many of these people are dispersed persons and have given up affiliation with the mainstream denominations, but are associated with the smaller and sometimes more spiritual groups (of which there are many) awaiting the Parousia. The special people are the salt of the earth. They are performing a function of preservation which no other group can claim. But for them, the prophecy of Peter would have already come to pass and the earth would have melted with fervent heat.

Each group, depending on the confessed purpose, likes to think that they are the last Reformation. But there is sufficient indication in Holy Writ to give guidance as to what constitutes the particular characteristics of the Church and it is up to the individual to pay regard to the requirements which will satisfy the impartial, immortal Judge in the day of reckoning.

Because the special people being discussed here are called upon to be separate, are separated from the world and have left the city of destruction for another destination wherein dwelleth Righteousness, they have put away certain rivalries considered laudable but which are steeped and brewed in self. They are conscious of the high calling. Instead of busying themselves building echelons, they follow the rule not to think more highly of themselves than they ought, *"in honour preferring one another"* (Romans 12:10), thanking God for success when it is achieved by others and praying for others in the circle as though the prayers concern themselves, hoping that every gift bestowed within the circle will be used for the praise of the Giver. Jesus said:

> *Ye know that the princes of the Gentiles exercise dominion over them, and they that are great exercise authority upon them. But it shall not be so among you;*

but whosoever will be great among you, let him be your minister; and whosoever will be chief among you, let him be your servant (Matthew 20:25-27).

The special people, like Abraham, are characterized by faith. They have come into the Kingdom by "saving faith" with which they have more than a passing acquaintance. They, however, must fall within the category referred to in the Scriptures which says, *"the just shall live by faith: but if any man draw back, my soul shall have no pleasure in him"* (Hebrews 10:38). God's honour roll is not a list of precedents in which protocol must be maintained in deference to the favour bestowed by the authority. It reposes on whether the believer can be described as *"full of the Holy Ghost and of faith"* (Acts 11:24).

The special people are required to *"shew forth the praises of him who hath called* [them] *out of darkness into his marvellous light"* (1 Peter 2:9). This vocation of praise is not an elective. Nor is it the hymn of praise and the words of service without the works of obedience. This has to be seen like the ship's manifest and be in accord with the cargo on board. It has to be marked in the code employed and must be capable of being identified with the bill of lading already in the hands of the Divine Surveyor at the port of entry.

Special therefore, is not special in respect to abnormalities but special in respect to regularity and function.

5. A MODEL OF MAN

THE MODEL OF MAN DISCLOSES that what was intended was secured. The product, however, was not a programmed automaton and the permanence of the achievement was in the hands of the creature. This masterpiece was of a very high order, *"a little lower than the angels"* (Psalm 8:5), but His Excellence gave him responsibility as well as choice.

It was upon a summer's day in a garden between the Tigris and the Euphrates when the quality of life changed dramatically in Eden by a blunder which was clearly warned against. And so we find ourselves having to deal with an Adamic species far removed from the created version, needing metamorphosis and remedial treatment.

Owing to the brevity of this work, it is not possible to have a full-blown discussion of unregenerate or Adamic man. It will be sufficient to say that Unregenerate Man wears an actor's mask (persona). He lost his clothes in his gamble in Eden and a borrowed cloak, the skin of a lower animal, had to be thrown to him gratuitously by his Maker.

This model faces Reality and is about the real person, the individual who is an entity without pretense or makeup. Its first and most basic assumption is that the redeemed, in the entirety of his being, is filled, animated or quickened by the breath or Spirit of God. The model begins with the creation story of the first Adam (Genesis 2:7) and reaches its high point in the life, death, burial and resurrection of the second Adam, the Lord Jesus Christ, of whom it was testified that He was the success story which the first Adam did not provide. He was *"full of the Holy Ghost"* (Luke 4:1) and came to do the will of the Father. This is the salient characteristic of the entire life and ministry of Jesus. It earns Him, after His resurrection, the peculiar honour of being *"the first fruits of them that slept"* (1 Corinthians 15:20).

The structure of the human person presented to us both in the Old and New Testaments is that of body, soul and spirit. Man is made in the image of God (Genesis 1:26,27). He is made to be the temple of the Living God. This is not an idea presented for the first time in the New Testament as some authors suggest. It began with the creation. Man is both material and nonmaterial. The statement in Genesis that man was made in the image and likeness of the Divine raises the question of whether he was formed complete with body, soul and spirit; that is, whether he was given a spirit of his own prior to the infusion of the breath of God (Genesis 2:7). Viewed with the clinging mystery of "the image and likeness," some say that tripartite man refers to the pre-operative status; others, that it relates to the post-operative status of the finished work. The debate will not be developed here, however, since what is most important is not whether there is a "spirit of man" as distinct from his soul but whether or not the man gives his allegiance to God and whether or not the Spirit of God is resident in him. Even if Edenic man did have a spirit of his own, this spirit was to be totally subsumed, suffused and controlled by the Spirit of God.

The discussion which follows is illustrated in Figure 3 where man has been described from three perspectives. This chapter does not examine primarily Unregenerate Man under the control of his human, fallen or Adamic spirit. Rather, it seeks to understand Regenerate Man (see Figure 3, column 3), indwelt once again by the Divine and who reverts to the position existing before the Fall.

The eternal Spirit of God who transcends all creation is available to each believer. He enters the human dwelling place upon invitation; while His existence is independent of His creation, His influence is dependent on human receptivity. The spirit component is the most intangible and the most delicately consitituted part of man, yet it is the most significant. The spirit component, however, is the least permanent entity and it can be substituted for or replaced at any given time unlike its more corporeal partners. Sometime before birth takes place, the natural man receives a spirit. During the course of his life he will become aware that, in common with other men, his spirit is affected by the Adamic failure. He can, with the assistance of the Divine, have the spirit with which he was born substituted for and replaced or controlled by the Spirit of Christ. This is called the New Birth. What follows is referred to as walking or living in the Spirit. The Holy Spirit never departs from an individual unless he commits blasphemy and bids the Spirit to go. It is the Holy Spirit who brings a man to desire a change from the carnal to the spiritual. Upon His entry into the individual heart, the spirit of the "old man" dies; this is miraculously and supernaturally replaced with the "New Man," Christ Jesus, given to us by the Holy Spirit (Ezekiel 11:19). There is both a divestiture and an investiture. A replacement transpires. The New Man will not live with the old.

CREATED MAN	FALLEN MAN	REGENERATE MAN
(Genesis 2)	**Adamic Spirit** (*psychikos*, 1 Corinthians 2:14,15)	**Presence of Spirit of God** (*pneuma, pneumatikos, ruach*, 1 Corinthians 2:14,15)
Communion with God	Ungodly fear	Faith in Jesus Christ
	Vanity, Pride	Fear of God, Holiness
	Self-exaltation	Love of God, Power, Temperance
	Self-dependency	Peace, Light, Life, Virtue, Truth
Image of God	Self as idol	Wisdom, Knowledge, Compassion
	Self-condemnation	Meekness, Forgiveness, Dignity
	Self-depreciation	Joy, Long-suffering, Gentleness
Moral	Carnal behaviour	Goodness, Moral conscience and action
	Corrupt speech	Speech "seasoned with salt"
Pronounced "good"	**Dead Soul**	**Living Soul** (Hebrew: *nepeš*, Greek: *psyche*)
	Human will	Will - (submitted to God, 1 Thessalonians 5:23)
	Natural mind	Heart - the attitude of standing firm, affection, tenderness, seeking sanctified emotions, desires and appetites, zeal, conscience, attention, imagination, allegiance, judgement, understanding
	Carnal thoughts	
	Carnal desire	
	Carnal emotions	
		Mind - a guard, a close watch, thoughts, intellect, incipient attitudes, ability to perceive, discriminate, understand truth
	Natural Body	**Temple/Body**

(CHARACTER labels run vertically alongside CREATED MAN and FALLEN MAN columns)

Figure 3 - MODEL OF MAN

The Growth of the Person

No attempt will be made to define the Spirit of God in this model. This is better left in the cloud in which it is hid because of man's inability to describe the Infinite. What we do know is that the Spirit of God has some unfailing attributes—He is perfect in Holiness and in Glory. He is Absolute Light and Love and Life. He is eternal in His Omniscience, Omnipotence and His Omnipresence. He brings healing and joy. He is the Spirit of Liberty (Psalm 51:12; 2 Corinthians 3:17). Because He is love, He teaches us to reach to the other effecting unity which brings Peace. Together with peace, He gives Power. He gives Truth, along with inscrutable Wisdom and Knowledge. He ministers Mercy along with Grace. He is the just God who hates only sin—the monster of self which breeds division and death. In being Absolute Love and Holiness the Spirit of God expresses Moral Perfection. The Power He gives is not only of authority but also of virtue and courage. Where the Spirit of God is, there is no fear.

The mystery of God is unfathomable. It permeates not only His Person, but also His creation. Man himself is an extremely complex creature, *"fearfully and wonderfully made"* (Psalm 139:14).

The structure presented in Figure 3, therefore, does not do justice to the reality of man. It is merely a schematic representation of a being who is immeasurably intricate. A basic assumption of the model is that spirit integrates. When the Spirit of God is present in a man's heart, his entire being is affected—not only his heart. Unfortunately, the principle of integration is also true of the man ruled by the Adamic spirit in whom it takes the form of *dis*integration.

Simultaneous with this integration in the character of man's structure, however, there is a complicated dynamic interaction and overlap among the many aspects of his being. It seems to be a pervasive and permanent feature of the person that the different aspects of his being—"the soul," the "heart," the "spirit" have many attributes in common. This is indelibly and repetitively supported by Holy Scripture. To summarize what has been a lengthy search, we find that while the "spirit" has thoughts (perceptions) (Mark 2:8), emotions (John 11:33 and John 13:21), will, purpose (Acts 26:41, 19:21), the Hebrew word for "heart" (*leb, lebab*) also indicates reference to emotional states (1 Samuel 4:13; 2 Samuel 14:1), to intellectual activities such as attention (Exodus 8:23), reflection (Deutoronomy 7:17), memory (Deutoronomy 4:9) and to volition or purpose (1 Samuel 2:35). In the New Testament this pattern of overlap is repeated. The Greek term *kardia* (heart) retains the meaning of the seat of the will (Mark 3:5), of the intellect (Mark 2:6,8) and of feelings or emotions (Luke 24:32). The biblical translation "mind" also shares in these activities. For example, the word "mind" is used in relation to perfect peace (Isaiah 26:3), to willingness (1 Chronicles 28:9), to hardness of attitude (Daniel 5:20), to reflection (Luke 1:29), to vanity and pride (Ephesians 4:17; Colossians 2:18) and humility (Colossians 3:12). In general, the various uses of the word "mind" in the King James version of the Bible seem to suggest consistent reference to experiences that are normally construed to be of the heart or spirit. Turning to the term "soul," it appears that this word is used more often than not when the focus rests on the issues of life or death (Genesis 2:7; Psalm 33:18; Isaiah 55:3; Matthew 10:28; Hebrews 10:39). Even here, however there is overlap between the uses of "soul" and "spirit" (Acts 7:59).

For these reasons, it becomes very difficult to compartmentalize the human being. Perhaps we are forced to follow the tradition of the Hebrews who tended to avoid the modern error of overdepartmentalization. Some commentators advise that it was essentially the whole man, with all his attributes—physical, intellectual and psychological—of which the Hebrews thought and spoke and that the heart (*leb, lebab*) was conceived of as the governing centre for all of these. In this model, consequently, an attempt is made to preserve simplicity as far as possible. The "new" heart received by the Regenerate Man, as the seat of the total person, is in actuality an expression of the Spirit of God Himself. The thoughts, emotions and attitudes of the heart, indeed, the very will of the heart, are those inspired by the Holy Spirit Himself as Governor. It is His peace, His love and His truth that He brings to us.

Figure 3 does not pretend to be detailed in its scope. It is believed, however (see column 3, level 1), that it indicates the prime work of the Holy Spirit in the believer; that is, He produces in us a holy fear and love toward God. Holiness, as the first attribute of the Godhead, becomes increasingly characteristic of the individual. The Spirit of God brings us to the Father by giving us faith in Jesus Christ. A substantive contrast between the character regenerated by the Spirit of God and that spoiled by the Adamic spirit (see Figure 3) is that while the first is marked by power, love and a sound mind, the second is by nature tainted with ungodly fear often reaching the paralyzing proportions of anxiety and phobias. The Adamic spirit results in one of two extreme attitudes: either pride, vanity and self-exaltation or self-condemnation, self-depreciation and self-abnegation. Regenerate Man, however, is heir to dignity, not pride.

Attributes of the *imago Dei* at level 1 also include virtue, justice, courage, and the fruit of the Spirit described in Galatians 5:22. The fruit of the Spirit are infallible evidence of the experience of conversion in the life of Regenerate Man. He cannot take credit for this as it is a result of his adoption in the family of God.

While spirit as described in Regenerate Man is not identical with the Spirit of God, it is *of* the Spirit of God. A convenient definition of Regenerate Man, which may be better appreciated at this point, is the eternal, conscious breath of God (Greek: *pneuma*) or disposition (Hebrew: *ruach*) seen in the unfolding development of his character, which he cannot hide or mask, which identifies him, and which constitutes the causes for the changing aspects of his behaviour. The Spirit of God in Regenerate Man produces in that man, by His power, the capacity for maintaining a growing relationship with God through Jesus Christ.

In this respect, the regenerate believer prays for more of the Spirit of God who directs his attention to the Lord Jesus: *"For where your treasure is there will your heart be also"* (Luke 12:34).

At this level of the model, the Greek term *pneumatikos* (used on a few occasions by Paul to indicate Divine grace and its possession) is applied. It was carefully distinguished by Paul from the Greek *psychikos*, meaning man without the Spirit of God (see 1 Corinthians 2:14,15).

The second level of the model of Regenerate Man in Figure 3, described as the "living soul," takes its name from Genesis 2:7 but insists that man has been revived by the incoming Spirit of God. It is referred to throughout the Bible mainly by the Hebrew *nepes* and the New Testament Greek *psyche*. Of course, the term living soul infers that the soul may be dead. In the regenerate person, however, the soul indicates the total person endowed with the life principle; the seat of the emotions (Psalm 86:4; Isaiah 1:14), the physical appetites (Micah 7:1; Ecclesiastes 2:24) and is associated with the will and moral actions (Psalm 24:4; 25:1). In the Old Testament alone the word *nepes* has over fifty distinct meanings and is used variously to infer the heart, the mind, the desires, the will and the body. While Paul uses the Greek *psyche* along with *pneuma* to describe the lower and higher aspects respectively of immaterial man (1 Thessalonians 5:23), Peter uses *psyche* for the whole personality of man, reserving *pneuma*, in its human reference, for that part of man that survives death. In either case, however, there is no loss of conviction that the regenerate soul has reverted to communion with the Spirit of God and is under His complete control.

The attempt to simplify the description of the various functions and attributes of the Living Soul has resulted in reference to two main components—the heart and the mind.

The heart (Hebrew: *leb, lebab* and Greek: *kardia, zeteo* among other words) is understood as the center of the whole person, the inmost being. The will of the regenerate heart given by God allows it to "stand firm" in purpose and decision. Its emotions, desires and appetites are sanctified. So are its conscience, imaginations, allegiance, judgment, understanding and attention. The heart demonstrates affection, tenderness, zeal and is the more effective "instrument" in the eyes of God for seeking, searching and finding Him.

The English term "mind" in the Old Testament more often than not translates the Hebrew words for heart (*leb, lebab*) and is consequently given the same connotations. Other words, however, (for example, Hebrew *samar* and Greek *dianoia* and *nous*) lend additional and therefore distinctive meaning. On this basis, *mind* in this model is understood to include the modern term *intellect*—the ability to perceive, to discriminate, to understand the truth of God (see 1 Corinthians 14:15; 1 Corinthians 2:16; Luke 10:27; Mark 12:30;

Matthew 22:37). The mind also functions as a guard or a close watch (Hebrew: *samar*). Further, the promise of God for the mind is:

Thou wilt keep him in perfect peace, whose mind [Hebrew: yeserl = desire] *is stayed on thee* (Isaiah 26:3).

In order to reinforce its unquestionable inseparability with the heart, however, it serves to remember that the mind, in the language of the Scripture, bears connotations of cherishing, celebrating, expressing sympathy and compassion.

This having been said, it must immediately be acknowledged that this model seeks to clarify important and outstanding differences among the various components of the person rather than to focus on the many interesting similarities. For this reason, an attempt will be made to furnish a more detailed description of the mind and its functions as distinct from the heart. This is done since the mind, as the relatively modern term, appears to carry many more grey areas in popular usage and many more adaptations in biblical translation.

The mind of Regenerate Man (shown in column 3, level 2 of Figure 3) is not given to carnal thoughts. It is no longer natural. But it is still human. It is not perfect, but subject to the frailties of the human being. Though the regenerate mind is in submission and is at peace with the Will of God, it is not impervious to temptations coming either in the form of swift darts or in the hovering of ponderous, tenacious, threatening dirigibles (blimps). It is the Holy Spirit upon whom the individual depends in all these circumstances. He activates the mind which responds as a sieve separating the fine from the coarse. When the individual allows this operation to be effective it produces wholeness, or holiness. Ordinarily, the work-

THE GROWTH OF THE PERSON

ings of the individual's mind may be discovered in his thoughts, intellect, incipient attitudes and more comprehensively, in his behaviour. They are best summarized in the light of obedience to the Will of God. Amazingly, we are dependent on the Spirit of God even for this decisive strength.

The mind is the gateway or point of entry through which all non-substantial material must pass. These gates are not always open and blocks are sometimes erected there. In these circumstances, what is unwanted is dispersed. In other circumstances, the gate being open and the sentry unopposing, the goods enter and are unloaded on the premises for inspection or rejection as the case may be. This is the first port of entry into the man and he exercises the right to choose or to discard and to bring the sieve mentioned previously into use. The mind therefore, while not being equivalent to the spirit, is important.

In this model the view is taken, by way of repetition, that the mind of Regenerate Man, together with its will, is subsumed by but distinct from spirit. The evidence of this is the fact that, as a man the Lord Jesus, who was full of the Holy Spirit, could be tempted; but the Spirit of God within Him remained inviolate and performed the corrective function.

Obviously, the mind is more than the battleground for temptation. The meanings already itemized have disclosed that the mind is the framework for all rational activity which may be summarized by the modern term *noesis*. This includes human judgment, intelligence, memory, aptitudes, perception, cognitive style, cognitive invariant processes such as assimilation and accommodation, creativity. Concomitant with process, the mind also deals with content. Content categories include the individual's concept of God, self-concept, concept of others and concept of objective phenomena.

The emotions are not to be omitted, but they have their roots in the heart. It is understood that the emotions given to us by the Holy Spirit are stable and pure, for example, joy and love. It is posited that in Regenerate Man, the emotive and rational aspects of the personality are integrated and finely tuned by the Holy Spirit.

In Regenerate Man, the body is described as the temple of the Living God (1 Corinthians 3:16; 1 Corinthians 6:19) which is not to be defiled. The body, comprised of material substance, form and energy may be described in terms of the more specific attributes of physique, coordination, strength, dexterity, agility, endurance and force. It is the frail instrument through which the spirit and soul are expressed. *"But we have this treasure in earthen vessels, that the excellency of the power may be of God, and not of us"* (2 Corinthians 4:7).

The individual's constitution is understood as his genetic and inherited predisposition. This involves both the material and non-material person.

It is admitted that the discussion can accommodate several views leading in different directions, but in all of them—whether Calvinistic or whether it proposes that regeneration is renovation or implies replacement of the carnal man—the issue, the *"cause célèbre"* is Jesus.

In the beginning this was so. It is recorded that man was made in the image and likeness of God. The Father called upon His Son, saying: *"Let us make man in our image"* (Genesis 1:26). The prototype was Jesus. We read in the scholarly book of Hebrews that in the Incarnation the second Adam was made the express image of God, *"...so much better than the angels, as he hath by inheritance obtained a more excellent name than they"* (Hebrews 1:4). Here again, the issue is Jesus.

THE GROWTH OF THE PERSON

In the eschatological view of man it is written:

...and it doth not yet appear... what we shall be: but we know that when he shall appear, we shall be like him; for we shall see him as he is (1 John 3:2).

All the way from earth to heaven the issue will be Jesus.

With the Lord Jesus Christ as the key to the model of Regenerate Man, this work assumes the status of a model of Person rather than "persona." In Christ, we see the Person of God (*figura substantiae eius*) (Hebrews 1:3). This therefore, becomes a model of personhood—man as organized in the right direction toward God. It is a model which is intended to emphasize, like the Bible, not analysis but relationship.

PART III

THE DEVELOPING PERSON

6. A MODEL OF THE DEVELOPMENT OF THE PERSON

IN PSYCHOLOGICAL CIRCLES the development of the person has traditionally been discussed within two major points of view: stage theory and incremental theory.

Proponents of stage theory—such as Piaget, Kohlberg and Erikson in general developmental psychology and Dykstra and Parks, Elkind, Flavell, Fowler, Goldman, Oser in the psychology of religion—have exhibited interest in the approach which attempts to analyze the growing person's behaviour using sharp lines of demarcation. These imaginary lines create stages of development which are characteristically different and distinct, although each successive stage reputedly subsumes and reorganizes the characteristics of the previous stage. The demarcations are treated as being quite distinct. The alleged characteristics of each stage are highly contrastive. The names selected for each stage are even more so; for example, the Piagetian "sensori-motor" stage of infancy versus the "representational" stage of the young child approximately one-and-a-half to five years. Although this school of thought tends inevitably to put the growing child into iron-cast molds, it has been extremely popular in recent years.

Adherents of incremental theory argue that even if individuals did grow in recognizable stages, the fundamental and underlying basis for all movement, given the nature of human learning itself, would have to be incremental. Most disavow the validity of a theory that states that the individual develops in mechanistic jumps and starts. The incrementalists prefer to investigate the continuous, slow and undramatic development of the person rather than entertain the possible artificiality of "stages."

The present writer believes that it is ill-advised to "sneeze at" either point of view. Stage theory, with its nomenclatures, facilitates discussion. It also accommodates the human being's penchant for demonstrating phases, if not chiselled stages, in his growth. Whereas stage theory may be predominant in psychological theory today, however, there are many who would say that it is not totally beyond question. For example, although Fowler's theory of faith development, Kohlberg's theory of moral development and the cognitive Piagetian theory upon which they are both based by admission have all enjoyed remarkable popularity, the principles which have backed these theories appear to be straining at the seams. More important, the research which has supported them is now under fire on counts of poor sampling, lack of generalizability, inappropriate statistical methods and measurement techniques and faulty conceptualization among others.[15] Both Conn, in 1981, and

Bradley, in 1983, had reason to claim that Fowler's faith development theory was really concerned with knowing about faith in a Piagetian way of thinking, rather than with the contents of faith. The present writer adds that the processes and commitments of faith are also important and are certainly more significant than levels of thought. Spilka, Hood and Gorsuch in 1985 dismissed Fowler's theory because of its abstruseness, complexity and lack of empirical research. Kwilecki, in 1988, criticized theories of faith development such as Fowler's which did not allow for the great variety found on the single continuum of religious development (see, for example, Glock and Stark's five different dimensions of religiousness and Smart's six dimensions). With respect to the Piagetian theory, the barrage of criticism has never ended and is now even more severe. One category of critique which seems to strike right at the heart of the validity of his stages is the contention that the inability of children from four to six to comprehend a "conservation"[16] problem is related not to age and immaturity but to their unfamiliarity with the test materials and the language used. Along similar lines Holland and Rohrman concluded, in 1979, that "animistic thinking"[17] was not a genuine phenomenon but was due to linguistic confusion during testing sessions elicited by distant or novel objects and unfamiliar words.

In the context of the present discussion, the author's greatest concern regarding the Piagetian theory involves Piaget's epistemological concepts of "physical experience" and "logico-mathematico experience." Both concepts relate to the two-way interaction between the object and the learner. The first, physical experience is an attempt to describe the effect of the object on the learner's senses through his acquaintance with its colour, size, texture, shape and all other physical properties. In physical experience, the changes that occur with the child's age are simply more of the same, that is, there is more and more incoming data. In logico-mathematico experience on the other hand, qualitatively different mental processes characterize the new stage which is itself dependent on the learner's maturation. Thus it is the learner who acts on the object. For example, through a logical process the young learner suddenly "understands" that his familiar play blocks have acquired a "new characteristic." They will always total six in number whether they are pushed into a circular arrangement, re-ordered as a triangle or spaced in one straight line. This is not an action of the object but of the learner. This action of the mind on the objects provides a new insight, a *weltanschaunng*, a whole new vista, a new way of seeing the world which will forever remain with the child. It lifts him into a new level or stage of being. In Piaget's thinking, this action is too contrastive with the quality of the previous mindset to be incremental. The child either has the logical gift or he does not. It is the author's opinion, however, that whereas the flash of insight itself may be sudden, the essential process of acquiring logico-mathematico experience is still based on a slow, integrative, often laborious augmentation of facts which take place quietly, unobtrusively, without fanfare and which is no less important than the moment of "insight." No doubt Piaget would have agreed with this. After all, he conceded the possibility of a threshold effect, that is, the unpredictable occurrence of accurate responses on the part of the child but which the child still could not explain logically. What Piaget would perhaps not go as far as to agree with is that the traditional lines drawn between incremental learning and stage acquisition are merely figments of our imagination. Is it possible that the moment of insight, with respect to any given new behaviour, is itself always only the composite of a series of

THE GROWTH OF THE PERSON

related and/or tangential insights, so small that they may be dubbed incremental?

It is urged that the growing person who is regenerate and therefore "walking in the Spirit," will and does have a spiritual experience which is essentially both incremental and dramatic or characterized by stages of growth. Further, there is no need to separate the two processes since they complement and support each other. While the child's psychosocial development is constantly plagued by the vagaries of the social environment or the shortcomings of the human pedagogue, forcing entry into new psychosocial stages to be delayed or precocious, problematic or abrupt, in his spiritual development, God the Holy Spirit is unerring and available at all times, upon request, to lead into all truth. And He does so in limitless ways. Quite understandably, the incremental flow or the dramatic change in spiritual development may often be disturbed either by the person's stubborn will, or by the demands of a new situation which is given wrong priority. This can transpire, however, only if the individual takes his eyes away from the Teacher.

This much acknowledged, it must be admitted that God often deals with His people by passing them through greatening light in which divine revelation dawns upon them suddenly and gives them a delightful illumination not hitherto enjoyed. This is not peculiar to the dispensation of grace. There are many instances where the Lord, under the dispensation of the law, manifested His *shekinah* glory. The question of inspiration or divine guidance is expected to be a growing experience of the child of God until he is endued with the redemption of the body and life everlasting.

There are other propositions to be made with respect to spiritual development. Both psychosocial and spiritual development are subject to uneven growth patterns marked by unfortunate regressions. In this respect they are quite unlike intellectual development which tends to be continuous, without regressions, unless there is severe physical damage or trauma of some kind to the brain. Regressions are rarely simplistic. The person who arrives at point B and regresses to point A is not the same person that he was when he was first at point A. He takes back with him all the loaded wisdom or wantonness of his previous journey. The teacher encounters a new creature.

Unlike psychosocial development, spiritual development is fairly unrelated to chronological age and is not necessarily bound by intellectual limitations. In fact there is often an inverse relationship between intellectual development and faith. It often seems at times that as the individual grows in mental acuity and hardiness, he loses much of the spontaneity of a childlike faith. The Age of Reason has taught us that the rational is always the sworn enemy of faith, and that the measurements glorified in one realm are not necessarily applicable to the other. The intellectual basis of most psychological theories of development, therefore, should never be seen as the supportive platform for spiritual growth. The mark of the spiritual person is not "formal abstract thought" but faith in Jesus Christ; not "post-conventional moral reason" but faithfulness to God and to His Word; not "ego identity" but identity as a son or daughter of God; not mental exercise of one's faculties, but exercise in the discipline of prayer; not the building of character through self-determination and enlightenment but the acquisition of character through dependency on God and unqualified obedience. In fact, the requirements of spiritual growth are so diametrically opposed to those of the other aspects of the human being, taken together or separately, that it is frightening to imagine what the human person, without the Spirit of God, might really be.

MODEL

The model of development of the person being introduced is illustrated in Figures 4 and 5. This model, proposed by the present author, is intended primarily to describe the essence of the human person or personality as the individual develops, and to clarify the true nature of the inner man.

In keeping with the model seen in Figure 3, Figures 4 and 5 adhere to the view that the entire regenerate person is the temple of the living God. The Spirit is therefore not only the essence of the person but operates as the central control and may be represented graphically either by the innermost concentric circle or the outermost circle; that is, either as the core of the person or as the all-encompassing essence. Either way the symbolic representation carries an appropriate message.

The model respects Allport's distinction between extrinsic and intrinsic religion. It favours the sincerity and internal change of the intrinsic approach.[18] In this respect, it is really a model of relationship and not a model of the kinds of attitudes and presumptions which have given religion a "bad name." Relationship necessitates the presence of Person and its lifeblood is faith rather than ritual. It is in faith, the vehicle of Spirit, that we find the true man.

In view of the preceding, development, as described by psychological theory, must play second fiddle to faith. Research findings in psychology which are so volatile, may or may not be supportive of the model as the model itself must be faithfully based on development as described in the Bible. This is so for a number of reasons.

1. As previously discussed, the human being is primarily spirit. The individual's level of spirituality is therefore a more accurate description of the whole inner man

than the quality of his mind. It is important to note that "spirituality" as used here denotes the individual's entire style of life in relationship with God and man and as inspired by the Holy Spirit.

2. Ordinarily, psychology omits consideration of the most significant component of the definition of spirituality, dwelling only on the social to the exclusion of the transcendent.

3. Using psychological theory as the first backdrop for a model that includes religious components of man would serve little purpose since a) the evidence for general psychological theory is still often suspect and highly contradictory and b) the empirical support for psychological theories dealing with faith development is even more sparse and inconclusive. In many cases the theories themselves are so one-sided that they simply cannot be extended to spiritual development.

4. Psychology is notable for a paucity of sound, precise and discrete definitions of terms. This position is unfortunately exacerbated in relation to the psychological concept of "religion." For the Christian, the definition of "religion" and "development" must adhere to scriptural grounds and must remain uncontaminated by the confusions embedded in psychology. These terms must be seen clearly not as ritual but as salvation, indeed, as following Jesus Christ who said, *"...go and sell that thou hast, and... come, and follow me"* (Matthew 19:21).

5. Faith must be based on revelation and experience, not merely on cognition and cognitive skills.

6. A Christian model must be based on the sequence, recognition of sin, repentance, salvation. This

sequence of events is not found in Fowler's faith development theory,[19] nor is it elaborated in any psychological theory of development known to the author.

7. An individual's level of cognitive or social development may be greater than or less than his level of maturity in faith. Whatever the proportion, it is faith that is critical for the Christian.

Attempts could be made to construct hypothetical profiles for fictional individuals in order to illustrate the subtle interactions between spiritual levels of development and traditional psychology levels. This in fact is quite appealing. In doing so, however, we find that we can go only so far with theorizing. Psychological research is far too indeterminate and its results, if not its premises, still too dubious or contradictory to assist to any great degree. What, for example, is the nature of the relationship between "authoritarianism" and different forms of religion? What is the relationship between various forms of religion and self-righteousness, "self-esteem" or the "self-concept"? What of the Eriksonian dimension of trust/mistrust and religious experience? In the realm of the psychology of moral development, while Hyde[20] suggests that an autonomous faith must precede higher types of morality, Fowler takes the view that moral stages precede faith.

In all these questions that seem to matter so much to the enquiring type, we find that psychology is too often silent on the issue. Further, whenever some effort is made to decipher personality profiles and the fathomless connections between spirit and mind, we realize increasingly that it is the spirit and spiritual interpretation that counts—that in describing some incomprehensibly complex aspects of mind, we are really looking at spirit as it permeates mind, and that ultimately, if we are to describe the spirit adequately, at some point we must touch every aspect of the person.

This can probably be best illustrated by turning back temporarily to a discussion of the research on extrinsic religion and authoritarianism. Although this research has not been done exhaustively by any means, certain concessions may be made. Hyde (1990) attempts to summarize the psychological research done in relation to the extrinsic orientation to religion. He presents a fairly lengthy list of personality variables which correlate with the extrinsic orientation and consistently provides use of references. Among the list of correlates are evasiveness towards responsibility, prejudice, authoritarianism, little desire for independence and freedom, suspicion, competitiveness, low self-confidence, self-indulgence, indolence, propensity for the analytical as opposed to the wholistic, open-mindedness, inaccurate self-perceptions. A theological case could probably be argued for the relevance of each of these and the other variables in his list. Taken as a totality, it is easy to see that there is a noxious vein (of evil) throughout. To name only a few, prejudice is the intolerant attitude of those who feel they are superior to others and who make hasty prejudgments. Authoritarianism connotes little respect for the other person, among other things, and, theoretically, reflects on the self-image. Suspicion is a correlate, whether subdued or exaggerated, of fear of others. The sum total of all of these variables strongly suggests that "extrinsic religion" is in fact inspired by an evil spirit. We are reminded of the wise old saw, "the devil's playground is religion." But these variables constitute the everyday stuff of psychology. They are the standard fare of researchers in the field of psychology. It is with these very characteristics or their benign opposites on the relevant continua that psychologists have attempted over the decades to construct personality syndromes.

Could it be that psychologists, unbeknownst to them, have all along been dealing with the peripheral products of spirit—that they have been engrossed either with the specific machinations of the intrusive Adamic spirit or with correlates of the fruit of the Spirit of God? In fact, it would appear that in order to account for all the personality variables that have been studied over the decades and the many points on each continuum, at least two separate sub-models must now be developed to illustrate the disintegration due to the Adamic spirit and the integration afforded by the Spirit of God.

In continuing to reflect on the real but limited relevance of psychology to the spiritual, we realize further that whether a person is extremely sociable—that is to say outgoing and gregarious—or extremely reserved, whether the person is lacking in cognitive skill or is unnervingly precocious and intellectually brilliant, whether the person is emotionally expressive or obviously quiet is of little importance. If spirit is the center of personality, what matters most is whether the person is turned toward the holy or the profane, whether the person is walking in righteousness or in the flesh. These are the factors that enhance or confound natural inclination, native talent and idiosyncrasy. These are the factors that liberate to growth or that confine the person in the prison house of turmoil and disintegration. These are the essences that truly interact with mind and that result in the constructs—some horrendous, some beatific—studied by psychologists. Family/school environment, peer pressure, religious affiliation—all the well-known variances studied in developmental psychology are not the real issue. They are merely the contexts in which the real issues may be discussed.

It could be concluded that the most urgent need is to identify those behaviours, attitudes and traits which are of the flesh and to avoid them like the plague. This author suggests, however, that in the grave business of growing up, the only sure route is to identify the Author of Righteousness Himself and to follow. Self-sufficiency and self-dependence always slump into recession.

In keeping with all of the preceding, the model in Figures 4-5 attempts to secure conformity with the Word of God, defying gravitational pull and Euclidean theory, needing no props, admitting the advances which have been made by scientific scholarship but claiming to throw greater light on the subject of development. It is on record that some scientists devoted to the study of *Homo sapiens* have unwillingly reached the conclusion that *"the things which are seen are temporal; but the things that are not seen are eternal"* (2 Corinthians 4:18), and that, *"the glory of the celestial is one, and the glory of the terrestrial is another…"* (1 Corinthians 15:40).

Man is a trinity and in order to understand his person we must take into account his origin, his earthly existence and his destiny. Psychology as such has been largely concerned with the intermediate only—his existence.

The basic structure of Figure 3—body, soul and spirit—reappears in Figure 4 as entity and is represented by a set of concentric rings which assume different description depending on where the transverse takes place. The expressions of the entity subsume all aspects of personality including those discussed in psychology. The spiritual dimension explicitly represented by the innermost of the concentric rings provided, is elaborated on the right in Figure 4 since it is the influence of the spirit which determines the phases of development.

The graphic in Figure 4 takes an irregular shape. The transverse at B is wider than that at A since it can be assumed that just prior to salvation, the individual has a greater sense of need and is experiencing some "divine discontent" with his structure. Disintegration is therefore greatest at this point. In the event of "spiritual awakening" and subsequent to it, there is an equally dramatic convergence and integration of the dimensions of personality which pass through three major identifiable phases up to the point of spiritual maturation marked Integrity.

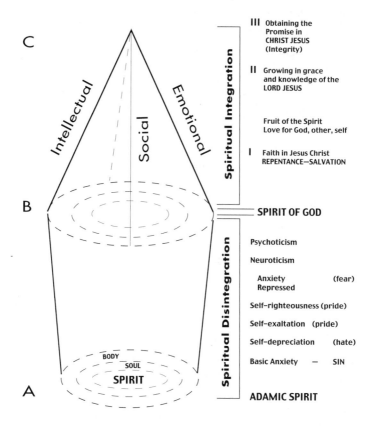

Figure 4 - DEVELOPMENT OF THE PERSON

The major stages in Figure 4, of which there are three, portray, first, the personal disintegration which results from the Adamic spirit. This is often quite subtle and deceptive, but one sees the effects in the confusion which exists both in individual lives and in the world at large.

The term "spiritual awakening" is used to describe the experience related in John 3 which is not necessarily of short duration, because people have varying degrees of urgency and some are known to postpone the claims for decision at personal peril almost over a lifetime. The specifics of the awakening are understood fully only by God Himself. It refers to the person's confrontation with the fact that he is a sinner or that everything in his disposition is contrary to the Spirit of God, his subsequent repentance or refusal to accept that condition, and his acceptance instead of God's grace. This entire experience is made possible by the work of the Holy Spirit. Properly speaking, it is only subsequent to this spiritual awakening or rebirth that true development begins. Spiritual rebirth also marks the termination point of personal disintegration. Essentially, it signals the death of the "old man" and the birth of the New Man, Christ Jesus.

Stage 2, phase 1 of Christian development is marked by faith in Jesus Christ as personal Lord. This faith, inspired by the Holy Spirit, paves the way for right relationship with God. Relationship is expressed as love for God first, and secondly for self and others. The task of describing the work of the Holy Spirit is difficult and well beyond man's feeble competence. We do know from the Scriptures, however, that the presence of the Spirit of God is accompanied by life-changing experiences (2 Timothy 1:7). Elsewhere, we are told that the Spirit of God gives us specific fruit in our lives (Galatians 5). These experiences are related in phase 1 to the individual's grounding in correct doctrine: the doctrines of repentance from dead works, faith towards God, baptism, laying on of hands, the resurrection from the dead and eternal judgment (Hebrews 6:1-3). As fundamental and far-reaching as these doctrines are, they are regarded by the Apostle Paul (Hebrews 5:12-14) as the *"first principles of the oracles of God"* and as the *"milk"* which must be substituted later by *"strong meat"* or the ability to discern both good and evil.

Phase 2 of Christian development involves the maturing of the individual as he grows *"in grace, and in the knowledge of our Lord and Saviour Jesus Christ"* (2 Peter 3:18). This period of testing and growth must of necessity be marked by patience, diligence and hope. The Christian is told not to be slothful but to be followers of them who through faith and patience inherit the promises (Hebrews 6:12). He has need to be alert, for the adversary the devil goeth about seeking whom he may devour. There is a prescribed route, however, for personal development which is carefully laid out in 2 Peter 1:5-11. The recommendation for obtaining spiritual character is:

> *...giving all diligence, adding to your faith virtue; and to virtue knowledge; and to knowledge temperance; and to temperance patience; and to patience godliness; and to godliness brotherly kindness; and to brotherly kindness charity* (5-7).

It could be argued that the parable of the seed sown by the wayside is a portrayal of the losses that may occur in phase 2 if disciples are not thoroughly rooted in the faith and doctrine of phase 1.

The maturing person of phase 2 is one who exercises gifts given by the Holy Spirit. As a member of the body of Christ, the Church, each believer is given one or more of nine gifts (1 Corinthians 12:4-11).

The outstanding characteristic of phase 2 relates once again to the Person of Jesus Christ who, as Saviour, protects, heals and nurtures.

Phase 3, "Obtaining the Promise," is epitomized in the believer's entry into the presence of God which will definitely occur after death. Experience of His *shekinah* glory should, however, begin in this life through the auspices of our Great High Priest who is able *"to save to the uttermost"* and who *"ever liveth to make intercession"* (Hebrews 7:25,26) for us. The hope that the Christian has of *"entering within the veil"* (Hebrews 6:19,20), is made sure by the fact that Christ, his forerunner, has already taken his place. The *sine qua non* of this phase is victory over sin.

It will be clear from the description of the preceding phases that this experience of Christian development is not at all comparable to the developmental process spoken of by MacMain in his 1980 research.[21] In studying young adults involved in local churches, MacMain discovered an interesting set of types. Some of the young adults still acknowledged the experienced faith of their parents, some clung to the faith of the church to which they belonged, some raised doubts and questions and moved into a searching faith, a few had worked through their commitment to an owned faith and a few others were still confused. Obviously, these types are largely resonant of those described by Fowler in his "Stages of Faith" and, perhaps to an equal extent, are reminiscent of the stages of identity outlined by Marcia (1966).[22] While this classification does point to real people and to real experiences, neither Marcia, Fowler nor MacMain has captured the essence of the development under discussion in this model. MacMain is noting the variation existing in faith based on differences in intellectual or cognitive assent, but the developmental phases set out in Figure 4 relate consistently to the total involvement of the whole person in the embrace of the Lord's Christ.

This contrast is also relevant to many other attempts to examine stages of development. It becomes particularly noticeable in the case of theories dealing with moral development. Neither Gilligan nor Kohlberg, for example, has succeeded in lifting moral development to the realm of consecration to the Person of God, but have both left it meandering on the plains of logical or affective experience imbued with human self-sufficiency; that is, the psychological theories are more concerned with exalting the supposed potential of the creature than with acknowledging the personal attributes of his omnipotent Maker. Thus the theories remain on the ground, terrestrial, denuded of their divine resources. The problem is not really that many theories treat the issues of love and justice as if they are mere abstractions. Indeed, since any act of justice must by nature pay attention to the particular person with his particular need in his particular situation, justice can never truly be abstract. The real problem is that it is sometimes forgotten that God *is* justice and God *is* love and we attempt to do what He alone is capable of doing. A discussion of these virtues as the ultimate goal for a universal ethic cannot be incorrect. The defect in the theories is that they allow love and justice to be assigned to the presumptuousness of human minds and to the frailty and incompetence of human hands and hearts.

Persons in any of the three phases of Christian development described in this model will demonstrate varying profiles due to their individualities or their idiosyncrasies. This will depend on levels of intellectual development, sociocultural patterns and education among other factors. All Christians, however, irrespective of background and experience, must exhibit the character of Christ. This is the true meaning of integrity.

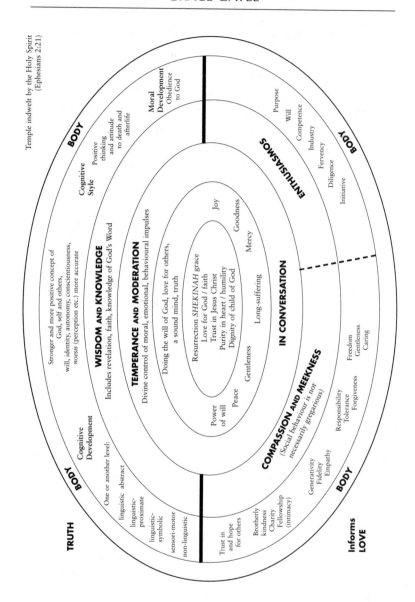

Figure 5 - CONSTITUTION OF REGENERATE MAN:
RELEVANCE OF PSYCHOLOGICAL CONSTRUCTS TO BIBLICAL EXPERIENCE

The constitution of the regenerate type is sketched in Figure 5. This figure attempts to explain the concentric rings of Figure 4 at the locus of integrity, enlarged for viewing. It represents the character of the whole person; that is, the expressions of entity which are realized in heart, mind and behaviour. It is understood that the body, as the temple of the Holy Spirit, reflects the holiness of the inner man but that in so doing, its colour, physique or stamina are largely irrelevant.

The concentric rings of Figure 5 are not intended to convey different levels of development. Their chief purpose is to display levels of specificity in describing Regenerate Man. A secondary function is to attempt to explain the relationship of some of the more well-known psychological constructs and terminology to biblical experience. Hence there is a progression from terms that are solely biblical at the centre, to biblical terms that seem to elucidate the basic psychological dimensions of the intellectual, social, moral and emotional, to terms that are predominantly psychological. The assumption that the model bears is once again seen in that the individual will only be integrated as he is thoroughly committed to the Person of Christ and is obedient to the Spirit of God (John 14:23). In Christian theology, the positive view which may be taken of man under these circumstances contrasts sharply with the nature of man ruled by the Adamic spirit.

The person represented by the sub-model of Figure 5 desires, and is totally dependent on, the presence of God and on the *rama* Word of God as given to the individual by the Holy Spirit Himself. Reference has been made earlier in this work to the *shekinah* glory of God. Many believers can testify to this supernatural visitation. Some have experienced the Baptism of Light without recognizing its special feature and its historicity, but all have come under the Spirit's sweet sway. Others speak exclusively of the baptism of the Holy Spirit with signs following or of the experience of sanctification while in this corporeal body and before their demise (or after, as in the case of the Catholics). Even those who state that they receive the Holy Spirit at their conversion and that there is no second definite work of grace will admit the return of the radiance of the presence of the Lord in exceptional miraculous ways during their pilgrimage. What the author is saying, here, is that personality cannot be explained in the lives of teeming millions of regenerate people without reference to the miraculous. And its omission will leave the subject observably incomplete.

The individual may be described in his innermost being as imbued with love and Godly fear. This is made possible by his faith. Faith here is understood in its broadest meaning. That is, in keeping with its Greek equivalent (*pisteuo*), it indicates not just belief in the Father, the Lord Jesus Christ and the Holy Spirit, but giving of allegiance to the triune God, as well as appropriate action. It is a verb denoting continuous activity, not a noun declaring an abstract, static, infertile concept. Above all, it demands obedience. The presence of God implies that the vessel has been cleansed and the heart is purified—a return to the status enjoyed prior to the Fall. The first evidence of this will be the presence of the fruit of the Spirit in the believer's life (indicated in the second concentric circle). This is manifested in the desire to submit to the will of God, in the presence of peace, love, a sound mind and the more specific attributes of long-suffering, joy, gentleness, goodness, mercy and truth. The individual believer also receives power to live victoriously and to resist evil.

Temperance, also one of the fruits of the Spirit, has been positioned in the third concentric circle as it needs special attention and explanation. It is the *sine qua non* linking the first and second circles to the fourth. It is the refinement of the biblical term "self-control" used in modern versions of the Bible. While the expression "self-control" is used extensively in psychology, its correct biblical meaning is control under God (Acts 24:25; Galatians 5:22,23). A most interesting English translation of the original Greek word for temperance (*enkrateia*) is found in 1 Corinthians 9:25 where, in the metaphor of the Christian race, the athlete preparing for the prize is said to exercise self-control in all things or to "go into training"; that is, to subject himself to training on a systematic basis. It is worth noting that other English synonyms for temperance are moderation, calmness, lack of extremes. Temperance, with all its apparent variations in meaning, may require complete abstinence, moderation, or complete devotion unto righteousness. In this model it is summarized simply but meaningfully as divine control in behaviour, conduct, deportment or manner of life (represented in scriptural language by the term "conversation"). Because of its necessary all-pervasiveness, moderation will characterize the regenerate person not only in respect to wisdom and knowledge (see Figure 5), but will also be evident in expressions of compassion and meekness as well as the subconstruct referred to as *Enthusiasmos*. It is therefore realized that all expressions of temperance should be actuated not only in outward observable behaviour but also in internal behaviour (thought).

The scriptural injunction towards temperance in one's "conversation" is believed to have first application to the individual's moral and emotional behaviour. (Moral development and behaviour have been discussed and will be further examined in subsequent paragraphs.) Emotions are effusive thought which may or may not be accompanied by bodily expression and behaviour. They may be positive or negative. Emotional development is the process by which feeling is cultured, disciplined or trained and allowed to express or not to express itself. This involves a combination of 1) perception of what is appropriate; 2) temperament or the individual's inherited patterns of response; 3) control to bring behaviour in line with what is perceived to be appropriate, often in defiance of or in contrast to natural temperament. One of the highest examples of emotional maturity and the goal to which every Christian should aspire, may be seen in the incident where Jesus healed the soldier's ear in the garden of Gethsemane (Luke 22:50-51). Here the Lord, even in His passion, demonstrated kingly deportment, meekness, gentleness, love, absence of strife and retaliation, humility, patience and thus dignity. Neither is there any suggestion that He had to subdue contrary inner feelings for He was filled with the Spirit of God. Since the biblical view holds that we relate to the Godhead primarily through our emotions rather than through "head knowledge," this model accords a dominant role to the emotions in the three innermost circles.

The dark lines used in the fourth and fifth circles of Figure 5 are an indication that 1) the biblical terms "wisdom" and "knowledge" are superordinate to the more specific terms used in the upper half of the fifth circle; 2) the biblical terms "compassion," "meekness" and "*enthusiasmos*" command the more specific terms in the lower half of the fifth circle; 3) the two sets of superordinate terms are not directly interrelated but are related primarily through the intervention of the Spirit of God (Proverbs 9:10; Proverbs 1:7; Galatians 5:22-23).

It is important to understand that the wisdom and knowledge imparted by God are not based altogether on intuition and reason but on faith and revelation. Whereas intuition and cold reason are ordinarily experienced and depended on by all men, faith and warm revelation are the gifts of God to the regenerate. Whereas intuition and reason are often unsatisfactory and dubious (for example, a syllogism which obeys the rules of formal or pure logic often conveys no meaning), faith and revelation, given to the believer's heart, are precise and accurately on target. Whereas intuition and reason are totally dependent on, and will never exceed, the individual's level of cognitive or moral thought, faith and revelation, based on absolute truth, are entirely stable and are easily adaptable and informative to the individual's level of cognitive or moral development.

Altogether, the biblical terms of ring number 4 of Figure 5 include, but represent much more than the classic psychological dimensions of the intellectual, moral, emotional and the social. Further, in many instances, strong modifications must be made to the psychological concepts of the fifth ring before entry to the sub-model may be usefully made. A closer look at the fifth concentric ring will reveal that it represents a medley of psychological and religious/biblical terms. Though these terms are peripheral to the figure, they are by no means unimportant, for they go a far way toward a comprehensive description of the day-to-day expression of the Realities found in the central circle.

With respect to the upper half of the fifth circle, what is considered to be the most important component of wisdom and knowledge has been placed at the top portion of this section— that is, an accurate, positive concept of God. In child development the infant has a primitive self-concept before he acquires a concept of God, but he cannot have a proper concept of self and of others in later life unless he becomes aware of the Higher Authority. Further, it is absolutely necessary for the individual to see both his neighbour and himself as having inestimable worth or value in the eyes of God. It has been said that truth informs love. An understanding of God, therefore, the highest possible form of knowledge and wisdom known to man, facilitates all other forms and gives direction to the love and respect for God, self and others implied in the lower half of the fifth circle. Closely associated with the individual's self-concept is his "identity," a psychological concept which refers not only to how the individual sees himself and perceives himself to be seen by others, but also to the individual's sense of his place in the world, his ideology, his career goals, his personal ambitions, his reason for living—perspectives that are so personally private that they cannot be lived or perceived by another. The "will," though not of the same fibre as wisdom and knowledge, is closely influenced by them. It should have overtones of the strength of character necessary for the exercise of temperance. The struggle involved in bringing man's will into alignment with the will of God requires the help of the Holy Spirit as seen in the emotional energy/restraint necessary for temperance, compassion and meekness; that is, for the psychological term "will" to be accepted in this model and take its place in the fifth concentric circle, it must be understood in relation to the biblical term "power" of the second circle.

Psychological levels of moral and cognitive development must now be addressed more fully. This model acknowledges that the development of the whole person is primarily contingent on, and directed by, the spiritual—which, though closely correlated with, and affected by, the moral and the emotional, is to a large extent independent of both the physical and the intellectual. To illustrate, it has been stated that spirituality at the highest level refers to "Obtaining the Prize" (see Figure 4). The acid test for this status in Christ is *victory over sin*. This is the *sine qua non* at any stage It may be argued that a young, egocentric child of 3-6 years, who could hardly have the cognitive maturity to demonstrate understanding for the needs of others, may yet be at this phase of moral maturity. The truth which inheres in such a situation is that, while intellectual understanding may be necessary for empathy, it is not a prerequisite for the spiritual and moral experience of compassion. Further, the model presents the view that even where understanding is lacking in the young or the old, Christ, the Good Shepherd, leads His sheep in paths of righteousness and peace, and tends the less mobile young in His bosom. (In the Exodus, the children of Israel were commanded not to walk faster than the young children could walk.) It is therefore possible to find many combinations of levels of spirituality with varying levels of cognitive/intellectual development, types of cognitive styles and maturity of *noesis*.

The moral and emotional, then, are closer to the spiritual when properly defined. It should be borne in mind that the morality of the regenerate person is measured by his submission to the will of God and is quite distinct from the morality of the world. In many instances, the world seeks to blur differences between opposites and often makes, to popular acclaim, the infamous famous.

"Cognitive development," as used here, refers in part to the well-known Piagetian stages which remain helpful indices—though not error-free, as illustrated by the weaknesses previously discussed. In addition, the author wishes to suggest a general modification to the classic Piagetian stages, on the basis of the fast-growing evidence that logical behaviour does not begin in Piaget's third stage, that of "concrete operations" (approximately 6 - 12 years), but that infants have their own sensori-motor form of logic.[23] The greatest cognitive change during childhood, on the basis of this author's belief, is not one from non-logical to logical behaviour but rather from non-linguistic to linguistic behaviour; thus, the following major phases in cognitive intellectual development are proposed: sensori-motor non-linguistic intelligence, linguistic symbolic intelligence, linguistic proximate (or concrete-operational) intelligence and linguistic abstract intelligence. Obviously, in this context, the sensori-motor phase is outstanding since it will seriously impede the proper acquisition and articulation of one's faith. For this reason, the experience of "spiritual awakening" or rebirth" is humanly impossible at this phase. It is best, therefore, to refer to the spiritual realities of this phase in the simple terms of the immanence of God. The assumption here is that unless rebirth occurs in the succeeding phase, the individual child will be increasingly and visibly influenced by the Adamic spirit.

The term "cognitive style" is defined in the language used by Witkin as:

> ...characteristic modes of functioning that we show throughout our perceptual and intellectual activities in a highly consistent and pervasive way ("The Role of Cognitive Style in Academic Performance and Teacher-Student Relations" Research Paper).

Since cognitive styles by whatever name are usually presented as contrasting, dichotomous features on a continuum of their own, the point to be clarified here, theoretically, is that the spiritually-developed person is not necessarily found on either extreme of the continuum nor even necessarily at its mid-point. For example, the spiritually mature person is neither necessarily extremely field-dependent (gregarious, non-analytic, wholistic, etc.) nor necessarily extremely field-independent (withdrawn, analytic, linear, etc.) nor even necessarily a combination of both. The features of this dimension, as those of other cognitive styles, are simply not germane to spirituality. They have no identifiable correlation with holiness. Although psychological theory has attempted from time to time to equate opposite extremes in cognitive style with maturity, this model firmly renounces any significant correlation between spirituality/holiness and intellectual/cognitive development.

The term "moral development" (the ability to distinguish right from wrong) is used here in a way which requires serious reflection regarding Kohlberg's theory. This author is aware of the many criticisms which have made of Kohlberg's theory in psychological literature as well as of his distinct contribution to the field. The debate has revolved largely around the fact that Kohlberg's proposed levels of moral development—the preconventional (or heteronomous), the conventional and the post-conventional—are embedded almost exclusively in the dimension of formal moral thought (that is, the reason adduced for one's action). This is at the expense of other dimensions of moral development such as the ability to correctly resolve a problem over and above its rational demands (the administration of justice), the ability to identify cultural and other values entrenched in the problem and the individual's strength of will to translate decisions into behaviour. To this list may be added the individual's particular ethic of conscience (whether duty, loyalty, love, virtue or law, see Richard Taylor, [24]). Many have questioned whether Kohlberg's sixth substage—universal ethical principles (primarily justice)—is in fact biased and one-sided (for example, void of emotional content).

In order to avoid unnecessary debate and confusion, this author wishes to state here and now that Kohlberg's theory, to the extent that it may be so, is ultimately adequate only for the unregenerate. Unlike the Kohlbergian view that cognitive development precedes and is the basis for moral development, the view taken in this model is that spiritual experience, the key to the entire personality, must precede true moral development. Research done by Mischey (1981) among others, seems to agree that an autonomous faith might be a necessary condition for higher (autonomous) types of morality.[25]

In keeping with the emphasis on the regenerate person in the sub-model of Figure 5, it is believed that when the Spirit of God is in control (this includes the cases where the person is in early childhood), levels of formal moral thought (the reason for action), which may be related to heteronomous rule of an authority figure or group or to autonomous rule by the self, become definitely subordinate to the rule of God. This is in keeping with the view that faith is supreme and may often supercede reason. Faith, being transcendent, also provides a check-balance in the event that the society or group or individual becomes degenerate. On the dimension of behaviour, the decisive index of moral development, the regenerate person recognizes that moral development does not tolerate degrees. An action is either moral or immoral. The believer is either obedient or disobedient to the will and Word of God. Many claim that it is not easy to determine the difference between right and wrong because of the prevalence of large "grey" areas. But it is believed that when such occasions arise, the believer is notified by the Spirit to *stop*, *look* and *listen*. If this is faithfully adhered to, direction can be obtained.

The surrender of "pre-conventional/conventional" referents as a basis for moral thought in no way implies, however, that the rational is absent in moral development. Indeed, since the regenerate person is relatively more integrated, thought is of utmost importance to morality. It is therefore suggested that what is needed is the admission of a very different type of thought. Instead of the growing person contemplating morality solely in terms of this or that benefit to himself or others, he, if regenerate, will be directed to think in terms of faith in God, obedience to God, compassion, meekness and worth—the very substance of the lower half of Figure 5. These are the biblical factors which make relationship between God and man possible. The first and highest criterion will always be the consideration, desire for and commitment to holiness. This is the true essence of morality. This escapes the humanist.

In this context it is useful for us to remind ourselves that Christ, the head of the Christian Church, was *the* most holy and yet most *un*conventional person who ever lived. It is inconsistent, therefore, for His true followers to be blindly attached to any cultural norm, institution, authority or society.

The question of moral development in this sub-model, therefore, may be summarized simply but seriously as obedience to the Word and Will of God. Although the educated person may be aware of cultural practices and professional, social or other norms, it is the will of God which remains the deciding factor. The model adheres to the view that God's will is absolute. To the extent that the individual is dedicated to Christ, to that extent will his person and actions breathe the essence of morality. This does not make the individual a perfect person yet. He must continue striving to the end.

Kohlberg's model is highly rated. There are other models of moral development which have varying defects, but the same criticisms and conditions could be deduced. Whereas Kohlberg and some others relegate autonomy to the end of the individual's development, for the regenerate person autonomy is the rule throughout his Christian experience. This autonomy is surrendered to God.

The overall outcome of biblical wisdom and knowledge is an attitude of purpose towards living, a life filled with discipline (cf. *discipulus*) as a disciple of Christ and a positive attitude to death and the afterlife. This surpasses the Eriksonian concept of integrity by leaps and bounds. Above all it is noticeable in the Latin translation of the New Testament that the word used for the servant of God is not the more highbrow term "minister" but is the common garden term *servus* (Philippians 2). On this note we pass to the compassion and meekness of the lower half of Figure 5.

Just as the fear or awe of God inspired by the Holy Spirit is the generative force behind the realities of the upper half of Figure 5, so too the love of God, indicated in the central circle, emanates to the lower portion of Figure 5. If compassion and meekness are attempted without the presence and the love of God Himself, they become mere strategies of man's mind which soon begin to strain at the seams. There can be no true love for man without love for God. Nor does love for one's neighbour precede love for God. Rather, it is the presence of God and our faith in Him (obedience) which makes possible the expression of love toward our neighbour.

The most significant origin of the portion of the model referred to as "Compassion and Meekness" is humility. The importance of this virtue springs from the fact that it is found as part of the character of God the Father. The love of the Father is not a draining, taking love but a caring, giving love. In fact, it is notable that the Father's love expresses a unique humility. Although there is none whom He must obey, and although He is incomparably high and great, yet He humbles Himself to take note of the things which are created. The humility of the Lord Jesus shows a unique duality. While He also exhibits the gentle care for His children, He also gives us the example in being obedient at all times to the will of the Father. In this His self-sacrifice is supreme.

Humility is also synonymous with lamblikeness, dovelikeness (peaceableness) and with meekness. The term meekness (Greek: *prautes*) means primarily gentleness, (2 Corinthians 10:1; Galatians 5:23) and Greek *praus* (Matthew 5:5; Matthew 11: 28,29) translates meek. Other instances of meekness in the life of Christ, particularly in His crucifixion, also connote absence of retaliation and self-justification. It is therefore with these qualities of the Spirit—obedience to God, gentleness, care, compassion and absence of self-righteousness—that the Christian must face the world.

As expected, the majority of the concepts under "Compassion and Meekness" summarize an orientation which is other-directed. Absorption with self is alien to the Spirit of Christ. The Christian should, without ostentation, demonstrate trust in and hope for the best for others. He should believe in the goodness and good intentions of others within the limits of godly understanding and wisdom and should be concerned with maintaining pure, positive relationships. Obviously, brotherly kindness, charity and service are attributes of the compassionate person, as well as responsibility, greater nearness to others and tolerance which have been found in a lengthy list of correlates of an intrinsic orientation to religion compiled by Hyde. The Eriksonian achievements of "trust," "intimacy" and "generativity" among others, with their corresponding virtues of fidelity, love and care, cannot be overlooked. In a model which is primarily Christian, however, some of these derivatives in psychology deserve serious examination. For instance, the term "intimacy" should be understood within the limits of holiness and fellowship and the term "generativity" should not be confined to procreation but should be interpreted to include any activity that will enhance the lives of others. This latter view was intended by Erikson himself.

Other attributes mentioned in this portion of Figure 5 also require special explanation. Ordinarily, "forgiveness" sounds appealing, humane and seems to be the sane approach to take. In this model of the person, however, the regenerate individual realizes that it has precise theological import. The Christian is to forgive others so that he may be forgiven by God. "Freedom" is not the latitude to do whatever appears to be pleasing or self-enhancing. Nor is it the liberty to self-direct. Rather, it is construed as the right to do what we ought to do and indicates to the believer the absence of bondage to sin and of ungodly fear of others. "Empathy," because it is based largely on understanding, is a dubious candidate for a list of indispensable attributes. It is strongly suggested that the first gift of God is not the empathy of the intellect which requires experience and perceptual maturity (a quality extensively examined and promoted by psychologists) but rather the more basic condition of the compassionate heart.

Because of its root meaning (*en* + *theos*), *enthusiasmos* has been accorded a superordinate position in this model and relates to a number of emotions including hope, joy, anticipation and the passion of mission. It is believed that it shines best when positioned in the lower half of Figure 5, since it is a driving force in the personality and is more compatible with the outward orientation of this section. It also summarizes the attitudes of competence, fervency, industry, diligence, purpose and initiative which are familiar in the language of psychology (Erikson, in one theory alone, has been able to suggest a logical and cohesive system for explaining many of these). These terms, however, are fully backed by scriptural usage and terminology. The Christian is exhorted to be *"not slothful in business but fervent in spirit, serving the Lord"* (Romans 12:11).

It is admitted that one may say something important without feeling. When an idea is clothed with passion and spoken with the zeal it deserves, things take on new meaning. For instance, it is not hard to see why the law at Sinai was given with thunder and lightning—so that it impressed the audience. The picture of the regenerate or integrated person presented in Figure 5, therefore, itself an expression of human effort, does well to be retouched by the following statement:

> *The first man Adam was made a living soul; the last Adam was made a quickening spirit... The first man is of the earth, earthy: the second man is the Lord from heaven* (1 Corinthians 15:45,47).

Integrity, which characterizes the totality of the meaning conveyed by Figure 5, is primarily a description of holiness. Whereas for Erikson it denotes equanimity in the face of death, absence of despair, and the ability to review the past with satisfaction and gratitude, for the Christian its first implication is the wholeness derived from walking in the counsel of the Almighty. *"And... God... breathed into his nostrils"* (Genesis 2:7).

The record here is very profound. Every theologian I have come across would be humble enough to admit that the process is beautifully described but not fully understood. Many thinkers have, however, decided to deride this statement and treat it as fictional. In doing so, they have lost the force of the epic.

When animals and plants breathe, something happens environmentally. In a spiritual sense, this is also true. The Psalmist says in his own inimitable way, *"Let everything that hath breath praise the Lord"* (Psalm 150:6). It is interesting to note that the Edenic breath of God referred to in the beginning, recurs with potency several times thereafter in Scripture. Jesus breathed upon His disciples and said, *"Receive ye the Holy*

Ghost" (John 20:22). Prior to that Elijah breathed upon the Shunamite woman's son and he was restored to life. This question of breath will not be put down and is of greatest importance in the life of Regenerate Man.

God's breath is life. This is what the model seeks to acknowledge. This is what was given to man in the Garden of Eden as His chief bequest. The miraculous breath will take place suddenly but there is a lot of room for growing in grace. These graces will not be acquired overnight. As the person experiences enlightenment and tastes of the heavenly gift, his responsibility, which was featured in the Edenic scene, increases (Hebrews 6:4-6).

PART IV

DISPARITIES

7. INTRODUCTION

I̲n̲ ̲t̲h̲e̲ ̲w̲o̲r̲d̲s̲ ̲o̲f̲ ̲t̲h̲e̲ ̲L̲o̲r̲d̲ ̲J̲e̲s̲u̲s̲ ̲C̲h̲r̲i̲s̲t̲, the One who fully knew the rigors of temptation—who *"was in all points tempted like as we are, yet without sin"* (Hebrews 4:15)—the devil *"cometh not, but for to steal, and to kill and to destroy"* (John 10:10). There is no need to wonder how this may be done. The most obvious and calamitous strategy which he uses to effect this is to divert man's attention from God. Without our attention where it should be, there is no perception of divine glory, no worship, no obedience, an ill-conceived sense of self-sufficiency, an absence of the presence of the Spirit of God and, to top this formidable list of sins, a predisposition to do what one wants. This all leads to death.

In this section, the author hopes to convince the reader that psychology, like bodily exercise, "profiteth little" and cannot replace exercise in godliness. It is proposed that contemporary psychology, as it is known and applied in the Western world, has been, over the decades, the playground of detractors and currently constitutes one of the most brazen attempts to steal man's attention from God, like Walt Disney's little mascot Mickey Mouse who turns millions away from the real world. Unfortunately, to a large extent, countless millions have been caught in the grip of the great lie which affirms, *"Ye shall not surely die"* (Genesis 3:4). While its hypothetical theories and research methodologies have ventured far into the realm of truth and achieved some degree of cohesiveness, psychology, generally speaking, remains in the turmoil of confusion and error. In a disconcerting way it muddles causes with effects, tolerates oversimplifications, locates the "normal" as necessarily at the peak of a frequency curve and habitually uses sparse and often contrived findings to deduce that man is his own good cure for his ills. Despite the apparent ambivalence, he is well, he is hale and hearty, he is good and does not need the services of the Great Physician.

This psychology will continue to do, for, led by the Destroyer, it has managed consistently to circumvent consideration of man's true essence. Today, no one remembers that the lure of psychology is alien to the truth of man's origin and life; few even realize that the root meaning of the term psychology is the Greek word *psyche* (soul, breath of life) related to the Greek *psychikos* (1 Corinthians 2:4) that is, "the natural man without the Spirit," and almost everyone assumes that a psychology without interest in God can be corrective and healing. Almost no one, therefore, is alert to the vast discrepancies existing between the Word of God as expressed in the Bible

THE GROWTH OF THE PERSON

and the current dogmas of psychology which are rapidly becoming more and more popular. In saying this, the recent attempts of a few psychologists (e.g., those affiliated with organizations like the Christian Association for Psychological Studies) must, of course, be recognized. Unfortunately, these works have, for the most part, illustrated endeavours to "psychologize" religion rather than put psychology and psychotherapy on trial. There have also been a few brilliant attempts to confront some of the easygoing assumptions of psychology and psychotherapy with the Word.[26] Often, however, this is done without the support of a comprehensive investigation and presentation of man as revealed in the Bible.

The major objective of the chapters which follow, therefore, is to highlight some of the discrepancies between psychological theory and the Christian view of man held by the early Church, differences existing between science and revelation, and to note these differences within the biblical framework already provided by Figures 1-5. The true man of faith, though joyously accepting any psychological discovery which supports his point of view, cannot afford to be led by any hand away from the bastions of truth. While he allows room for science always, he believes that ultimately, science will prove to be the servant of revelation.

To achieve this objective, a series of psychological topics, issues, concepts, ideas and basic attitudes will be examined in separate chapters of this section, critiqued objectively and dispassionately but determinedly held before the searching light of the Gospel.

8. "Ye Must be Born Again"

WHEN NICODEMUS, A RULER OF THE JEWS, came to Jesus by night, he had one question on his heart: what was the gripping difference between Jesus and other men? How could the difference be reconciled? He came armed with a question but found himself making a statement: *"Rabbi, we know that thou art a teacher come from God: for no man can do these miracles that thou doest, except God be with him"* (John 3:2). What he did not, perhaps, express in words was the burning desire within him to participate in the life he saw in Jesus. As if fully aware of the secrets of his heart, Jesus does not speak of Himself at first, but addresses Nicodemus' need and his unspoken question: *"Verily, verily I say unto* *thee, Except a man be born again, he cannot see the kingdom of God* (verse 3). The non-verbal query which prompted Jesus' response is one which every unbiased person would have asked but which was not verbalized by anyone, even Nicodemus, because of its immensity.

The world does not admit the need for reconciliation, or even that a deficit exists. Likewise, psychologists have not yet dealt with the truth that, *"That which is born of the flesh is flesh; and that which is born of the Spirit is spirit"* (John 3:6). There are still many today who believe that grace comes from within them and that they do not need the death of Christ or the cross for the grace of God to operate in their lives. Those who say this, however, including many a psychologist, forget that the Greek word *sarx*, used for flesh in the New Testament and applied once more in this particular Scripture (John chapter 3), means not only carnal, sinful man but also man in the natural, following his own human standards. When Jesus says therefore, *"Ye must be born again,"* He is speaking to those who have yielded to sensual desires and corruption of the flesh. But He is also speaking to every man who has ever been born.

The "must" of this quotation carries a particular force. It is not intended as a piece of flattery, nor as a patronizing slap on the back. It is not a kindly request or suggestion. In fact, it is an injunction. The Greek which is translated "must" has the force of oughtness. Thus it is not the compulsiveness of those who cannot help themselves. It is operable only where the will is in place. It is a high summons before the Almighty, whose Spirit *"breathes where he desires"* (John 3:8; literal English translation of the Greek). Coming as it does from the mouth of the Divine, this "must" is not one of several alternatives which may or may not be adopted, but a serious exhortation which must be heeded by those who would be heaven-bound.

THE GROWTH OF THE PERSON

These are they who know that *Deus scientiarum dominus est* and who recognize that although the great masters of psychology have dissected the mind, analyzed it, torn it apart or sometimes left it as one, the real man—the living soul—is yet to be explained and accepted in the halls of learning.

9. SELF-CONTROL versus HOLINESS

THE DISCUSSIONS IN PARTS II AND III of this work on the soul of Adamic man present the indubitable view that his constitution is carnal. With the best of intentions, Adamic man will always contribute to error; although he knows that *"righteousness exalteth a nation"* (Proverbs 14:34), the strong likelihood is that by himself he will always be a reproach to his country and will always be a trouble to himself.

Man's greatest need, therefore, is found in Nicodemus' implied question, and its solution in the answer given by the Master.

Though carnal, Adamic man is imbued with the desire for nobility among men. His self-appointed answer to the problem is to strive for self-control. Invariably, this means the control of self by the self.

Unfortunately, in the realm of psychology, thinkers rarely, if ever, hold the Christian interpretation of self-control. The psychological concept of "self-control" is not to be ignored either as a point of scientific interest for research or as a long-term goal for education. It may even be said that self-control, with its twin concept, self-dependency, form the central core of the behavioural syndromes currently under investigation. The topic of self-control or self-regulation is pertinent, in one way or another, to most of the major theories in psychology. For example, it may be recognized in Freudian writings as well as in Bandura's "reciprocal determinism" or Rotter's "internal locus of control." If self-control is seen as synonymous with "autonomy," the familiar "autonomy/heteronomy" contrast, various aspects of which are seen in Piaget, Kohlberg, Fowler, Skinner, Rogers—to name only a few of the most celebrated theorists—also enters the picture. If self-control is associated with "self-actualization," the vast body of literature dealing with self-fulfillment, expressiveness, relationship with others and goal-fulfillment claims relevance.

A tremendous amount of thinking has been done on the topic of self-control. For example, Mischel and Mischel have organized the issues surrounding self-control into four major categories: a) delay of gratification, b) evaluative self-reaction and self-regulation, c) control of visceral and glandular responses, d) moral reasoning.[27] But these are not the only existing paradigms for research on self-control. Also to be considered is the voluminous research on speech disorders, hyperactivity, emotional disorders and delinquency among the network of negative phenomena.

What has become clear is that self-control and its converse elements (instability, compulsivity, neuroticism, etc.), now rank extremely high on a measure of significant topics in psychology. What has not been addressed seriously is the standard or standards which should form the basis for self-control. It would appear that in the hurry to propose and defend this concept, psychologists have come to accept the notion of relatives and the individual's right to adjudicate. Supported by psychology, it is now the popular belief that morality is every man's own standard. Little attention has been given to the possibility of absolutes. In fact, it even seems that the topic of self-control is now understood as alien to the existence of absolutes and more so to the existence of an ultimate Absolute. As explained previously, for many psychologists man is his own leverage, his own balance, his own god. In short, psychology simply does not recognize the necessity of holiness.

It is the opinion of the author that, important as it is, the concept of self-control needs to be removed from the cloud of misinterpretations in which it is hidden. First of all, it must be understood that self-control and God-control are not necessarily at opposing ends of a continuum. The real difference between the psychological and Christian perspectives on self-control is one of usage. While the humanist uses the term to indicate the control of the self by the self, the Bible uses it in a reflexive way to describe the control of the self by God with the full desire, cooperation and submission of the individual. It is rightly assessed, therefore, as a dynamic interaction. Second, the reality of divine control is not always easily realized for it may involve struggle against the Adamic nature. Should an attempt be made to describe this process in greater detail, the following four phases may be outlined.

1. The Holy Spirit "woos" us, leading us to Christ. That is, our initial approach is the work of the Spirit, not ours.

2. We love the Lord.
3. As we love Him, we keep His words (John 14:23).
4. As we continue to be obedient, we have immanence. God dwells with us, leading us into all truth and guiding us.

The analysis reveals clearly that throughout this process the individual is never just a puppet. He is no less active than the humanistic self-made man. There is much for the Christian to do. (Paradoxically this is so in spite of the fact that we can never earn our salvation which has already been paid for by Christ.) It may even be said that the Christian's submissive activity is a key to the entire operation of the Spirit. The individual who is under the control of the Almighty is never compelled. He is invited to yield to the will of God, but having done so, or simultaneous with this choice, there are various and certain tasks for him to do, attitudes to adopt, responses to make and acts of obedience to perform. It is believed that this view is strictly in keeping with the Holy Scriptures where self-control or temperance is a gift of the Spirit (Galatians 5:23), but also a command (Titus 1:8; 2 Peter 1:6). It must be confessed, however, that while self-control is at one and the same time an act of God on man and an act of man, it is primarily an act of God. It is God who gives the desire for His will to be done.

From the Christian standpoint, the real issue in a discussion on temperance inheres in the question - How much do we really love Jesus? True imitation of Jesus demands control by the Father for, after all, as Bernard said, the Master's life was "the mirror of temperance". *And every man that striveth for the mastery is temperate in all things.* (1 Corinthians 9:25).

In imitating Christ, the exhortation is not to trust in our righteousness which is as "filthy rags" but ONLY in His Righteousness. We must be covered with His Robes which are still "all of one piece", not our own.

10. THE REAL LIVING BEING:

PERSONALITY, SPIRITUALITY OR HOLINESS?

Names are often difficult to choose. Sometimes they are given because of a mere fondness for tradition. Sometimes they are almost happened upon because of the euphony of the word or the reminder it holds for a dear one. On more rare occasions, however, they have a meaning and serve a chosen purpose.

The difficulty with the human being is to find a name for him which is appropriate and a description which is fitting. On the surface, we seem to have many ways of discussing the human being. On closer examination, however, we find that each name, like the shoe that is being fitted, has its own peculiar problem. We wonder if the perfect fit will be found. What word or phrase correctly describes the true living human being, the one transformed from death to life?

The dictionary definition of "person" is, "any human being considered as a distinct entity or personality; an individual." An individual, on the other hand, is a "unit distinguished from others of the same kind." Theologically, person is said to mean one of the three individualities in the Trinity. Simply put, personality is that which is "of a person" (Funk & Wagnalls, *Standard College Dictionary*).

It is difficult, however, to justify the use of the term "person" or its derivative "personality" (both of which originate with the Latin word *persona* meaning an "actor's mask" or a "character in a play") to describe Regenerate Man.

Of course concessions will always be made and one may imagine that the term personality will continue to be used loosely and indiscriminately. But the term "personality" should technically be limited to those aspects of the unregenerate person which are shown as convenient contrivances in normal social interaction; it accommodates the reality that while the human being ideally strives for authenticity, it would appear that in many cases, social convention, cooperation, and popular caution are close rivals. In fact, inauthenticity may often creep in on the guise of improving one's sociability.

To take the problem further, many who practise the science of psychology will boast that they have indeed seen the dangers and pitfalls of the term "personality" unless applied, as it should properly be, only to surface congeniality and convenient strategy. The Latin term *persona* has been duly retained in modern psychology to indicate a personality assumed for the purposes of deception or concealment. Some of these scientists/theorists claim to have penetrated "behind the mask" and to have uncovered the true realities (Freud, Jung, Rank,

Binswanger, etc.). There is now even a popular psychology textbook entitled *Behind the Masks*. In most cases, however, their view of the realities behind the masks is just as dim as the spectral vision of the masks worn in the living theatres of this world. What the scientists have emerged with is a meagre handful of behavioural platitudes which they have attributed to the presence or absence of human self-actualization.

In the case of a demonic spirit, the root origin of the word personality (*persona*) seems very apt. When the Deceiver comes he does not show his true face but is capable of presenting many masks. This is seen nowhere more clearly than in the disorder known as multiple personality disorder (MPD). The master fiend, knowing that his presence will terrify and offend, allows his less frightening and seductive serfs, saturated and motivated by his sentiment, to beguile and captivate the victim.

It must hastily be added that the only Scripture in the New Testament (KJV) which uses the word "person" with reference to the Godhead is not deprived of its awe by this usage: *"Who being the brightness of his glory, and the express image of his person..."* (Hebrews 1:3). God has no masks. What we see happening here, therefore, is the simple interference of popular linguistic usage. Indeed, if the original term for person in this verse of Scripture is sought, we immediately find that the words used in Wordsworth and White's second edition of the Latin New Testament are the straightforward and wholesome expression *figura substantiae* (the image of His essence). The earlier Greek version of the New Testament also uses the equivalent of the term essence.

The proposition which should be developed is that the root meaning of the word person, though totally inappropriate for reference to Spirit, is relevant to fallen spirits. To proceed further, it appears that the expressions "spirituality" and "personality," circulated as companion terms in current jargon, are inventions of modern language. J.D. Douglas[28] claims that the words character, personality, will, mind, (disported for so long and currently prioritized in psychology), are modern terms which all reflect something of the meaning of "heart" in their biblical usage (cf. Hebrew *leb, lebab*). To further illustrate the intrusion of modern terms into the Scriptures, the present author observes that there was apparently no concept for the modern "mind" in ancient Hebrew. In Deuteronomy 6:5, the children of Israel are told only to *"...love the Lord thy God with all thine heart, and with all thy soul, and with all thy might."* Elsewhere in the Old Testament, the modern translation "mind" most often replaces the Hebrew words *leb* and *lebab*. The concept of mind was no doubt fully developed only with the advent of the intellectual Greeks, whose veneration for abstract idea led them to assign it the status of deity. It is doubtless due only to this development that the New Testament Greek reference to the first commandment (Mark 12:30) does include the concept *dianoia* (mind).

Turning back to the word person, we find that on most occasions when it is used in the Old Testament it is supplied only for clarity in translation. On almost every other occasion it replaces the Hebrew *nepes* (soul). In the New Testament, it replaces the Greek *soma* (body). In fact, etymologically, its Latin root proves its relative recency. While we would not wish to be guilty of Piagetian "linguistic realism" by assuming that the essence of a word is in its name, it is safe to deduce that the concept of person was not fully developed even at the time of the Roman civilization, and that it was much later absorbed into modern translations of the Bible to accommodate the popular lingua of our times.

The term "spirituality" seems to have its own problems in current understanding. One of these problems is its widespread usage to cover not only reference to the Christian religion but also to a variety of Western and Eastern religions (including Buddhism, Hinduism, Taoism) and practices (transcendentalism, spiritualism, etc.) which are in disagreement with basic Christian doctrine and experience.

The second and perhaps subtler problem is the confusion which has arisen (often aided and abetted by "giants" of psychology such as Maslow, Rogers and many existentialists) between the words sociability and spirituality. The term sociability has been wrested from the level of ability and introduced to the level of compulsion; it has been dissociated from compassion and allotted to gregariousness; it has been accorded godlike importance and set up against the virtues of holiness and restraint. In many quarters, instead of being secondary to religion, religion has come to be seen as a sub-category of the social. Often the concept of sociability is so idolized that persons low on the scale are evaluated as deficient in some way.

These aberrations make otherwise useful terms questionable. It therefore becomes necessary to redefine terms, apply them with caution, and appreciate them on the basis of their origins. In these circumstances, it is prudent to describe the regenerate or truly alive human being simply in terms of the process he has undergone, the purity of his thought and action and his knowledge of the presence of God. When this transpires, it is realized that either acutely high or extremely low sociability may be dangerous. In dealing with the priorities claimed by psychology, it must be remembered that sociability and affability do not necessarily arise from the love of God, for, unlike the indiscriminate concerns of the psychologist, the Christian knows that the wicked are often strong in character. And unlike the Christian's care for purity of heart, the psychologist continues to tithe the "anise and cumin."

Jacques Maritain takes the concepts of personality and spirituality beyond the level of the social. For him the term personality involves the notion of wholeness and independence:

> To say that a man is a person is to say that in the depth of his being he is more a whole than a part and more independent than servile. It is this mystery of our nature which religious thought designates when it says that the person is the image of God. A person possesses absolute dignity because he is in direct relationship with the realm of being, truth, goodness and beauty and with God, and it is only with these that he can arrive at his complete fulfillment (*Education at the Crossroads*).

In the face of Maritain's accommodation to the use of words like person and personality, and in the context of their historical usage by many another theologian, perhaps we should wink good humouredly at the etymological root of the words. Perhaps we should simply allow these terms to shed their original meanings and assume the highest possible connotations. The Creator has no shams or pretenses. He is the source of all true being, the great "I Am that I Am" whose essence is holiness. This is what the psychologist needs to admit because it is a strong disparity.

Further, if we are to lift the terms person and personality to the level of the supernatural, we must say that God is *the* Person, not *a* person. God is a Spirit, but He *is* Person. God is the Creator and origin of all personhood. This is why the devil, who has divorced himself from God, is death. Strictly speaking, there is no need to speak of the Person of God *and* the person of the devil. So far, psychology has insisted on discussing personhood and personality as the expression of the individual's uniqueness among other men. There is need for concentration on their proper meaning—participation in God.

It is noteworthy that while the Scriptures refer repeatedly to God as a Spirit, there is only one reference to Him as Person and this is in the context of the distinctiveness proper within the Trinity (Hebrews 1:3). There being no possible distinctiveness between God and those who are found *in* Him (that is, without God we are nothing), God's Word regarding the love relationship between Himself and man does not emphasize His being as a Person, but as a Spirit. God's message to His creatures is not one of distance or of distinctiveness but of unity in Him.

Since God is a Spirit, we would best speak of Him in terms of His attributes. Scripture never discusses the being of God apart from His attributes, inasmuch as God is what He reveals Himself to be. The many attributes found in Scripture give us a worthy impression of both His transcendence and His immanence. Though we could barely do justice to this topic here, and though we are all condemned to seeing as *"through a glass, darkly"* (1 Corinthians 13:12) it is rewarding to explore what J.D. Douglass has to say on the subject:

> ...the attributes of God belong to the very essence of His Being and... they are therefore coextensive with His nature. That is to say, in God attributes and being are one. This is not so in the case of men. The attributes of a man's character, because he is finite, are subject to limitation. In him there is a difference between being, living, knowing and willing, and the most we can expect is that they should be adequately balanced. In God His attributes are all-pervasive, and each of them is infinite and without limitation. For example, we cannot say that God is partly love and partly justice: He is all love and all justice. Each attribute is itself God, and God is fully expressed in each attribute. Then again, man remains

man even if he does not possess certain human attributes: God is not God without all His attributes...

Communicable attributes are qualities that can, in measure, be communicated to His rational and moral creatures, such as wisdom, goodness, righteousness, justice, love, that is, attributes that express the immanence of God. Incommunicable attributes are divine perfections which can have no analogy in human character, such as self-existence, immutability, omniscience, eternity, that is, the attributes that emphasize His transcendence...

It is not so much that God is everywhere; He is Himself the Everywhere. Moreover, He is wholly, and not partly, present everywhere... (J.D. Douglas, *The New Bible Dictionary*).

11. ASSURANCE VERSUS OPEN-MINDEDNESS AND CLOSED-MINDEDNESS

Both CLOSED-MINDEDNESS and open-mindedness are earmarks of the mind. Assurance emanates from the heart.

The question therefore, is not whether it is better to be open-minded rather than closed-minded or vice versa. For the professing Christian, the question is, does his faith stand on the solid rock of certainty and assurance or is he on the shifting sands of opinion?

Assurance is demonstrated in the annals of history. It is a cardinal feature of Judaism and is carried over to the Christian Church—one of its most important characteristics. This assurance was not acquired. This is how the Church was born.

No careful reader of the Acts of the Apostles can fail to see that the emphasis in this book is a declaration of what would become the constitution of the Church and the bill of rights of every member. It could be stated in different terms, but in any of the different modes in which the constitution is presented, the clarion call is assurance. All are struck by the fact that the founder of the Ecclesia was not looking for a formula or setting up another dogma. He was, as He stated and as corroborated in the experience of His disciples, *"the way, the truth and the life"* (John 14:6). People found this out for themselves. They were not asked to adopt a cliché, to make a pilgrimage or to offer an incantation. No creed or oath of allegiance was demanded. The assurance was personal, was arrived at independently and given on a basis whereby evidence could be seen and recognized as conclusive witness and testimony.

Perhaps it cannot be claimed that this experience is characteristic of all the denominational churches today. It may be said however, that as the hallmark of Christian experience, assurance will return to the Church as its blood-bought gift, before the return of Jesus Christ.

Assurance is not to be mistaken with feelings or even exclusively with emotion and certainly not with reason. It stems instead from confidence in the Other and in the certainty of His acceptance and His promises: *"In my Father's house are many mansions. I go to prepare a place for you and if I go, I will come again"* (John 14:1-4), or, *"Come unto me, all ye that labour and are heavy laden, and I will give you rest"* (Matthew 11:28), or, *"The Lord is my light and my salvation"* (Psalm 27:1). The Greek for John 3:16 brings out the position a little more trenchantly than the English. It says *"anyone believing into him shall not perish, but have everlasting life."*

Assurance is therefore not primarily belief in a fact but in a Person. It is the trust of the child who looks upward to the loving eyes of the One who cares, held in the arms of our nursing

Father (*El Shaddai*). Assurance is not secured by pronouncement from some potentate. It is a conviction given by the Master. The Evangelical Church believes that no one but the individual himself has been given the right to announce the gift received by the disciple on a one-to-one basis from the Lord.

To pass the test, assurance and trust must be accompanied by obedience. In doing so, the experience of assurance enters the realm of behaviour where other poignant attitudes arise. Assurance does not tolerate scepticism, wavering or double-mindedness. The apostle James warns that the double-minded man is as the *"wave of the sea driven with the wind and tossed,"* and, *" let not that man think that he shall receive anything of the Lord"* (James 1:6,7). In the same book (chapter 4, verse 8), we read that the double-minded person has a soiled heart and unclean hands; in short, he needs to resist the devil and draw nigh to God.

Over the centuries, Christian assurance has been seriously attacked on many sides. Perhaps the most subtle of these attacks, but certainly the one which concerns us here, is that directed by psychology. Over and over again, Christian assurance and faith have been confused in psychology with closed-mindedness. It is therefore important to set out a precise definition of the psychological terms "open-mindedness" and "closed-mindedness" and to attempt an unravelling of the present confusion.

In psychology, closed-mindedness is customarily set out in the context of a "sick" personality syndrome and as a correlate of authoritarianism and dogmatism.[29] Both these latter terms are fraught with frightening and negative connotations, as is the term closed-mindedness. In fact, all three terms are merely different aspects of a far-reaching personality disorder. The authoritarian person (cf. unlike the authoritative person) is that person whose inner self has been dwarfed, stifled and often killed by the dictates of an authority figure in a heteronomous relationship. He has sold his birthright of choice and liberty in order to gain the security of relationship with a favoured power on whom he depends entirely. Ironically, he is simultaneously resentful of this power which has tended to absorb his life. Due to forced patterns of living and thinking, authoritarianism is usually accompanied by prejudgments, stereotypical thought, narrow categories of behaviour and thought and immaturity. Lacking the experiential categories which nourish thought, the individual inevitably becomes unable to think, gullible, constricted, closed-minded and, ironically, dogmatic. The most outstanding features of closed-mindedness are narrow category breadth and an inability to see or tolerate opposing points of view.

The converse of closed-mindedness, open-mindedness, is often given favourable evaluation in psychology. The "open-minded" person is less dependent on the opinion of others, and is regarded as more mature, more tolerant and more flexible in thought. This assumption should not be made, however. It is suggested here that open-mindedness may simply correlate with lack of decisive opinion, impetuousness, impulsivity and lack of conviction. This view is supported by the literature on psychopathology where psychotics are said to be prone to vacillation, uncertainty and indecision. Therefore, open-mindedness cannot be labelled healthy with any certainty, as psychologists are prone to label it, but questionable at best.

In the context of the debate which continues to rage in one form or another in psychology regarding the appropriateness or inappropriateness of either side of this dichotomy, it is suggested that a new manoeuvre is necessary, a totally different approach. It is believed that the options cannot be settled at the level of psychology, for here neither alternative has the clear advantage. The proposal, lifted to the level of faith in God, is that the one who seeks health should strive neither for closed-mindedness nor open-mindedness but should be receptive to the assurance of sonship which comes from God.

It is at this point in the deliberation however, that psychology's affront bears its sharpest sting. First, the Christian has been condemned not only for his alleged dependence on others around him, but primarily for his allegiance to the institution of the Church and its exclusive authority. See, for example, Carl Rogers' denouncement of traditional Christianity. Here, unfortunately, it appears that there is more than a grain of truth and that many church members have fallen short of the "liberty" to which they were called (Galatians 5:1). But while all this may be so, it need only be remembered that true religion, true Christianity, is not fostered by legalism and institutionalism but by personal experience following the Master in fellowship.

Second, the Christian (particularly the evangelical) has been habitually placed in a single category and charged with all the negative characteristics customarily associated with authoritarianism. Dittes and Batson,[30] in an attempt to defend today's "universalizing faith" with its claims for greater maturity, tolerance and comprehensiveness, argue that persons with lower self-esteem who are immature are also more likely to seek closure on the important issues of life and thus to affirm the dogmatic answers of traditional faith. Fortunately, Hood and Morris[31] have seen the position more clearly and have suggested that Fowler needs to examine his assumptions and make room in his theory for maturity *within* religious traditions.

They understand that, in the realm of faith, maturity is not demonstrated by the dilettante but by those who show sincere passion and certainty. In the Christian faith, this is an inevitable characteristic of relationship.

What of the issue of the so-called "conventional"? Can the Christian afford to be conventional in any epoch? Meissner[32] thinks not. For him, conventional religion, as conventional faith and conventional morality, are immature and non-biblical. This is in itself quite correct. Quite properly, the conventional has been equated with low ego-identity, a harsh superego and guilt. Once again the evangelistic churches appear to have been exclusively labelled with all of these faults although there is, perhaps, no greater machinery for conventionalism than the "niceties" of humanism.

The present writer acknowledges that the Christian, properly speaking, cannot be a slave to conventionalism. The Lord Jesus was not. While it is recognized that certain tendencies towards the conventional and its corollaries may be seen in Evangelical churches, one wonders if the flexibility and open-mindedness of the "non-conventional" churches is in any way superior. Could it not transpire that these latter churches have acquired a rigid standard of no standards? To what extent may this have affected their commitment to the will and Word of God and to what extent does this brand of legalism affect their identity as sons of God?

The undergraduate looked up into the steady eyes of the professor. "So," he said, "assurance has nothing to do with the fool." "Oh no!" replied the professor, eager to make the point, his body bent slightly forward in the attitude of conviction. "Assurance may be first cousin to the meek and lowly ass but it has no connection with the stupid fool. It is derived from the security (Latin: *ad* + *securum* = *sine cura* = sure) which is found as we cease to stand afar and draw near instead to the High Priest *'with a true heart in full assurance of faith'* (Hebrews 10:22)."

Psychology has not been totally wrong in its assault. But neither has it been right in its dogma. Psychology traditionally blames religion for closed-mindedness and gives all the "credit" to the "open-minded." While doing this, it fails miserably in appreciating what assurance does in the life of the person it seeks to investigate.

12. Self-Concept versus Spirit

The notion of "self-concept," upheld by the phenomenologists in psychological literature (e.g., Combs, Fitts, Perky, Rogers), is no longer a minor default for, due to the accretions given to it by their colleagues and admirers, it has become a monstrous misconceptualization.

In psychology, the self-concept refers to all the images (opinions and beliefs) that the individual has about himself. This includes his view of himself, his view of how others see him and his view of how others think he sees himself. The perceptual gestalt is theoretically based primarily on the opinion of "significant others" (whether friendly or unfriendly) in the individual's environment—opinions which become internalized and often accepted as the individual strives to maintain stable relationships. The greatest threats to the self-concept, therefore, are the negative attitudes and beliefs of the adult "facilitator" on whom the child is dependent. Moreover, almost all, if not all humanists in the current dogma, and even some alleged non-humanists, will avow that the self-concept is located at or very near the centre of the personality.

By means of these hypotheses, current understanding has distorted the human significance of the self-concept and made of it a huge idol, giving it an exaggerated importance. Psychology's premises have successfully bred devastating confusion.

In attempting to place the self-concept at the centre of the personality, psychology and its adherents have created serious inroads into the truth and has challenged the Christian view of the human being. In the experience of the Christian, self-concept is not only not the centre of Regenerate Man (see the model in Figure 5), it is also not the centre of the unregenerate personality. In both models, contrary to the claims of the humanist and the phenomenologist, self-concept is an important but peripheral (and largely cognitive) creation of the spirit resident within the person. Nor is "spirit" as used here to be taken to mean William James' "little man within the man" who was debunked by psychology decades ago—the homunculus which "may creep into our discussions of the dynamics of personality and be expected to solve all our problems without in reality solving any" (Gordon Allport, *Becoming*). Instead, spirit is understood as true entity in the context of the clear demarcations and counsel given to us in Scripture. The long-held allegation that the origin of self-concept is social and external to the individual is refuted by Scripture. Its origin may be both external and internal. This is not the prime issue. The real difficulty is that the problem of self-concept is deeper than the social and enters the realm of the spiritual. Perhaps the social element only serves to exacerbate or confirm an already established fact. Ironically, the research findings of some in the field of developmental psychology concur with Scripture. For example, Jerome Kagan has expressed the view, based on his observations, that in the first hours of life, long before the neonate has differentiated self from non-self and therefore long before it is cognitively mature enough to have a self-concept, it already has a personality. It seems clear, therefore, that the self-concept is not the central motivating force within the individual but the cognitive and perceptual by-product of a power that is either integrating or disintegrating.

Once the propositions pertinent to Figures 4 and 5 of Part III of this work are accepted, a number of other conflicting beliefs concerning the self-concept which originate in psychological theory, must be questioned.

To begin with, if the centre of personality is not the self-concept but spirit, then both self-concept and personality lose their alleged resistance to change and assume instead a marked modifiability depending on the presence of spirit. The weight of the model in Figure 4 is that even the hard encrustations of a negative self-concept brought about by the Adamic spirit will roll away in the presence of the Spirit of God.

Second, the quality of the "good" self-concept as represented in psychology is highly questionable. What is wanted is not the usual self-reliance, self-direction, self-actualization and self-esteem of the humanist. Good as these descriptions may seem, if they are bereft of a sense of dependence and trust in God, then they are merely quasi-assurances: not products of good self-concept but of an inflated self-concept which emanates from the pit and which in actuality is no better than the miserable wretchedness of the negative self-view. We must always remember that

Satan's original fall was preceded by the greatest form of vanity—his self-exaltation. Likewise, we are told, *"Pride goeth before destruction, and an haughty spirit before a fall"* (Proverbs 16:18).

In scriptural teaching, the good self-concept is quite distinguishable. Its centre is the individual's concept of God Himself. As children of the "Great I Am," believers affirm themselves as entities under God receptive to His choice characteristics and see themselves as *"a chosen generation, a royal priesthood, an holy nation, a peculiar people"* (1 Peter 2:9). This self-concept is based on humility before God. Further, it is rooted in grace and in the courage of faith in God. Nor is it a view which the individual has to work at cognitively to maintain. It is a gift of the tender, loving work of the Holy Spirit Himself who helps the individual to overcome all adversity.

Third, the notorious "fuzziness" of many psychological theories has contributed to the present failure to maintain a clear distinction between "good" or "high" self-concept. The terms, used almost interchangeably, become the confused basis not only for theoretical propositions, but also for measurement instruments and for educational applications. The alternate use of the words "good" and "high" is prevalent in other fields, but because psychology must ultimately be related to virtue, a distinction is necessary. It is agreed that good should be high and high should be good, but this is not the case in human affairs, and people, driven by the popular mood, tend to forget this.

Few theorists take the time to note that an individual with an exceedingly high and even realistic concept of himself may be—and often is—shorn of goodness and is excessively evil. This aberration was observed in Germany's Hitler—a calculating, cold-blooded racist and an inhuman persecutor of the non-conformist; yet arrogant, bombastic and egotistic. Nevertheless, he went over well with the majority of the population for a long time. Whatever his faults, he was said to have a high self-concept; however, as it turns out, this high was not beneficent but malevolent to the nth degree. There were other historical figures of the same breed. By now, the world should be aware of the fact that charisma by itself, the power of persuasion and mob psychology, although flowing from an elevated perception of one's self, usually lacks the gentility of meekness and the humility of the good self-concept. The situation is even worse when the self-concept is high but inflated and not backed by realism.

The literature is saturated with the idea that an extremely large discrepancy between self-concept and ideal self-concept is symptomatic of ill health. It does not make adequate allowance for the person who, although recognizing a large differential between the ideal and the actual, has committed the difference to his Maker and is expecting Him to fill the fissures in the gap and to make adjustments as He sees fit. Admittedly, psychology is dealing with the natural, but it should by now be realized that the miraculous is excluded with painful loss.

Fourth, the ineptitude of the psychological view is illustrated once again at the level of antidotes for poor self-concept. One corrective for poor self-concept in the psychological literature is an endless list of strategies to be used during social interaction and classroom interaction and intended to improve the messages received by the person with low self-concept. This is not good enough. On one hand, the sensitive recipient is only too aware when strategies are being applied and is likely to have his poor self-concept reconfirmed. On the other hand, the problem of the self-concept is really a problem of the heart. The heart, man's relationship with God, cannot be cured by social programmes or strategies, for this relationship can never be subordinated to man's relationship with man.

The heart of man has been omitted from theory of the self-concept for far too long. In the realm of the heart, the seat of the self-concept, we find so much more material than just the mere rationalization of an actively descriptive mind. In the heart the individual tucks away all the ways in which he has been carelessly or unlovingly treated by others. It is in the heart that the individual senses most deeply all the "conditions of worth" placed upon him by others. Here, too, is sometimes bitter memory of failure and even of sin. Most of this "baggage" has been discussed at one time or another by psychologists without any real admission of its true location or its nature. What psychologists have not yet acknowledged, moreover, is the presence of the devil who accuses if allowed, who hammers away relentlessly at the human heart, creating havoc and tearing it to shreds.

The antidote for poor self-concept, therefore, the question of the corrective and the cure, cannot be truly found at the level of social interaction and intervention. Just as the heart will not be permanently lightened by a human smile, touch or word, so too it cannot be cured by self-praise, by "good thinking" or even by self-inflicted penance. Nor can it be cured by protracted confession as a subtle form of self-abnegation. This will only facilitate the repeated incursions of the accuser. The heart can only be cured by following the process set out in the Book of books.

As a corollary to the preceding, the concept "conditions of worth" may be explored further. Rogers is adamant that the facilitator of the person with poor self-concept can be of help only if all conditions of worth are abandoned and the person is approached with "unconditional positive regard." This involves a readiness to prize the individual himself as someone of worth even if an authentic dislike for his behaviours and opinions is acknowledged. This author believes at least two criticisms are in order here. First, the attitude of unconditional positive regard is not natural to the human being and can only be achieved by the grace of God. The possibility that the facilitator will succeed in loving the other at moments of irritation and frustration, complicated by his own personal problems, is indeed minimal. Second, it is an indisputable fact that God's love is without conditions, available to all and boundless in mercy (John 3:16). The human being will never have a good self-concept until he sees himself as God sees him, having limitless value and worth in spite of unworthiness. The paradox, however, is that even in God's economy there are conditions of salvation. The repentant person, once cleansed, is required to be obedient, to be faithful. While it is true that "God made no junk," it is also true that He wants no junk. Repentance requires decision, turning the other way. It does not brook vacillation. The conditions of fidelity are explained:

> *But whosoever shall deny me before men, him will I also deny before my Father which is in heaven* (Matthew 10:33).

and conditions of death: "*...the wages of sin is death*" (Romans 6:23). How does the psychologist hope to eradicate all conditions of acceptance if God Himself, in His wisdom, does not? Has this psychological position introduced another of the "soft pedals" responsible for so much of the degeneracy in our culture today?

To effect improvement in poor self-concept, therefore, certain firm recommendations are made. The individual must, subsequent to repentance and salvation:

1. "Gird up the loins" of his mind. Because of its incorporeality the mind has been thought of as an abstraction,

an asset, but fragile, whimsical and taciturn. This in actual fact is not the case. The mind is not passive. It is not like a weathervane. It is not a place of gambol or of frisk. The mind has a structure and while not corporeal, has features which are identifiable in the corporeal. So under the anointing of the Spirit, Peter was able to say, *"Wherefore gird up the loins of your mind"* (1 Peter 1:13). The girding of the loins denotes the warrior about to take up arms, or the workman preparing for an arduous task. The mind therefore is not a garbage dump either for the devil or for others. It is a gateway but also a checkpoint.

2. Submit himself unto God as the temple of His Holy Spirit.

3. *"Resist the devil"* and his emissaries (James 4:7,8).

The mind and its self-concept are ancillary. The Spirit is principal. The mind is servant, the Spirit is Master. The self-concept is only the gift and is not the centre of personality. It is itself entirely dependent on the Giver.

Self-concept, though a cognitive construct, is neither cognitively nor even emotionally but spiritually organized.

13. Congruence versus Godliness

In the Rogerian theory of personality, "congruence" is the ultimate point of a process which begins with two basic needs: a) the need to actualize our benign inner potentials which is related to the process of actualization, and b) the need for positive regard from "significant others" in our environment which will support a positive self-concept. This is related to the process of self-actualization.

With respect to our actualizing tendency, there is no need for us to learn what is or is not actualizing. As stimuli and events are perceived unconsciously below the level of awareness by a process of subception, the individual has the innate capacity to value positively whatever he perceives as actualizing and to value negatively whatever he perceives as nonactualizing. This capacity is known as the Organismic Valuing Process. It relates to experience at the most private and subjective level. Rogers regards the subjective aspects of experience, however, as far more important than objective reality.

Of the two tendencies, actualization and self-actualization, it is the actualizing tendency based on the Organismic Valuing Process which appears first in infancy. Even in the case of the adult, however, the self-trust which is the earmark of this tendency is more attractive to Rogers, who says:

> Experience is for me the highest authority... when an activity feels as though it is valuable or worth doing, it is worth doing... [thus I trust] the totality of my experience which I have learned to suspect is wiser than my intellect. It is fallible, I am sure, but I believe it to be less fallible than my conscious mind alone (*On Becoming a Person*).

On the other hand, the self-actualizing tendency, the second of the two to appear, is subsidiary to the first and is more closely related to objective reality. As the growing infant expands its experiential field and learns to perceive itself as an entity separate and distinct from others, the self-concept emerges. The self-concept is entirely conscious. As the infant continues to develop, some of the actualizing tendency proper to the Organismic Valuing Process is directed towards realizing the goals and abilities of the self-concept. There is a growing complementarity of the two processes.

As long as the child's conscious learned conception of himself (self-concept) remains consistent or congruent with the total experience of his Organismic Valuing Process, the self-actualizing and actualizing tendencies work in unison to fulfil his innate potential. This happens in the best of all possible worlds where significant others treat the child consistently with "unconditional positive regard." This concept was explained in the previous section dealing with the self-concept.

Theoretically, the problem arises when the child, finding himself in a hostile, pathogenic or unsympathetic environment, attempts to win security by incorporating or introjecting parental standards into the self-concept and consequently into behaviour. Should parental values conflict with the child's subjective experience (i.e., his Organismic Valuing Process), the child is tempted to construct an acceptable self-concept at the expense of his "felt" self. Thus incongruence sets in. The Rogerian theory claims that this lack of congruence between self-concept and the Organismic Valuing Process is tantamount to lack of genuineness and induces an absence of openness to experience.

Where congruence and genuineness are achieved, however, the individual becomes a "fully functioning person" with an openness to experience and an awareness of himself, others and the environment.

Maslow's contribution to the humanistic concept of the "self-actualizing" person is almost phenomenal. He proposes at least fifteen outstanding characteristics of self-actualizing persons including:

1. greater acceptance of self and others,
2. greater spontaneity and self-knowledge,
3. greater autonomy and resistance to enculturation,
4. greater freshness of appreciation and richness of emotional response,
5. greater frequency of peak experiences or mystical moments of absolute perfection,
6. greater social interest,
7. greater creativity.

For Maslow, unlike Rogers, the self-actualizing person must learn how to integrate his intrinsic, innate or humanistic conscience (similar to the Rogerian Organismic Valuing Process) with his introjected conscience (similar to his self-concept). Again, unlike Rogers, Maslow recognizes that in the healthy person the self-actualizing tendency is not necessarily riveted to, dependent on or even subsidiary to the fulfillment of all intrinsic felt needs. Instead, the higher self-actualizing or "being" needs sometimes emerge even after the lower "deficiency" needs for love, security and esteem have been severely frustrated rather than gratified.

Very few of us live in the best of all possible worlds. Very few of us are surrounded by totally "nurturing" others. If Rogers' premises are slavishly applied, we must encounter severe ceilings for self-actualization, congruence or wholeness.

The Christian view of self-concept, however, explained in the previous chapter, as well as the Christian view of (self-)actualization, overcomes all blocks to the development of personality. The Christian knows who he is. He may be:

> ...troubled on every side, yet not distressed; ...perplexed, but not in despair; Persecuted, but not forsaken; cast down, but not destroyed... (2 Corinthians 4:8,9).

As Henley put it, "Under the bludgeonings of chance my head is bloody but unbowed" ("Invictus" in *The Literature of England*).

It is believed that this is applicable even to the child. The Christian, therefore, will not experience ceilings to his development as long as he continues to walk in faith, for his self-actualization is rooted in God.

If Rogers' theory were simply explanatory without being judgmental, it would be fairly innocuous. Unfortunately, he insists on seeing the child's felt needs as necessarily benign. If this were so, the child's encounter with a receptive and nurturing environment and the ensuing congruence would be a happy and fortunate set of circumstances. But Roger's theory is not supported by Scripture.

Congruence *per se* is not incompatible with the Creator's desire for our happiness. As He imparts a regenerate self-concept, so too He imparts cleansing to the inner man and all his desires. The more correct argument, therefore, is that if the Organismic Valuing Process has been cleansed, it is no longer what it was before, for the old flag obscuring the loyalties has been lowered, and the new flag stating whose we are and whom we serve has been hoisted. It is now a question of sounding the battle cry and of marching in order. The Organismic Valuing Process implies that each man has his own standards based on his perceptions. The outlook of the ransomed is not this. There is one Lawgiver, one Standard, one Judge. All temptations, all incursions of the enemy, all assaults upon the Word of God are submitted to the Heavenly Father and placed under the care of the Captain of the Lord's hosts.

The difficulty, therefore, really resides in the fact that Rogers appears to accept the admissibility of hostile, estranged, aggressive and even perverted emotions in the catalogue of Organismic Valuing Processes. He appears, for example, to allow for the perception of hatred and aggression among siblings as normal and as actualizing.[33] The fact of the occurrence of these emotions, although negative, is not denied. But they do not occur in the regenerate person and should be limited to a discussion of the unregenerate. The travesty arises, however, that this is seen as normal in the child's development and is encouraged without regard to its effect either on the child or on the society in which it moves. The effects of hatred, for example, would be colossal—narrowness of vision and feeling, inner deterioration and death—and, if followed to their logical conclusion, murder would be in order. The verses Matthew 5:21-22 are informative. Is not this the scenario we find in certain countries previously described as civilized but in which there has been a breakdown and now kinsmen are turned on their brothers and are engaged in looting, raping and killing in the name of ethnic cleansing?

What the Christian treasures is not congruence *per se*. Based as it is on individual perception, congruence is open to misinterpretation, error and even perversion. What the Christian desires is a conscience *"void of offense toward God, and toward men"* (Acts 24:16). He desires the gift of cleansing not only for his self-concept but also for his personal needs, desires, feelings and ambitions. Only so does he achieve true wholeness.

This is the consuming passion of every believer, irrespective of age, health, financial position, intellectual capacity, status; it will occupy his attention from the time of his second birth until the hour of his transit to Paradise.

The danger of trusting feelings is eminently summarized by St. Paul: " *If your heart condemn you, God is greater than your heart"* (1 John 3:20), and by Martin Luther: "You should not believe your conscience and your feelings more than the Word which the Lord... preaches to you" (quoted in James Michael Lee, *Handbook of Faith*).

14. Faulty Extremes versus God-control

In spite of the desperate need for integration in the science of psychology, we are witnessing an unsettling compartmentalization in our psychological thinking and theorizing. It has been too long evident in so many ways. We see it in the drastic shifts from cognitivism to behaviourism where even the keenest and most searching mind finds it difficult to recognize, in either philosophy, a successful attempt at explaining the complexity of man's nature. To put the matter simply, the cognitivist traditionally divorces himself from consideration of the contingencies of reinforcement in the environment, while the behaviourist looks everywhere except in the subject's mind for cause/effect sequences. At a more specific level of theorizing, an abundance of schools of thought present themselves. The reader must remain open-minded and unattached, flitting from the hard dogma of "behaviourism," to the egotism of "phenomenology," to the almost idolatrous deviation of "social learning theory," and on, perhaps, to the conceit of "artificial intelligence," or the banalities of "information processing theory"—not that each of these schools of thought does not have its own peculiar contribution to make. But an over-abundant supply of energy directed on any one school is more than likely to produce an aberration of the truth.

This same tendency towards compartmentalization and dualism is found once again within specific theories. Within cognitive learning theory alone, the psychological literature generates an ever-increasing number of dichotomies. There are the concepts of field-dependence versus field-independence (Witkin), of impulsivity versus reflection (Kagan), of simultaneous versus successive scanning (Bruner), of wide versus narrow category breadth (Bruner, Gardner), of autonomy versus heteronomy (Kohlberg) and many more. In the field of cognitive developmental psychology, the broader realities of "dependence versus independence" are more often than not treated as if they are mutually exclusive rather than potentially complementary. Moving to the literature on personality theory, there is an equal profusion of questionable alternatives. Subjects are described as having "internal versus external locus of control" (Rotter), as being "introverted versus extroverted" (Eysenck) or as lacking or possessing "social interest" (Adler). Finally, on the behavioural level of real-life interaction, and as if in response to this simplistic if not "cock-eyed" use of opposites in psychology, we observe individuals adopting a dualistic disharmony and viewing themselves either with self-contempt or with pride depending on where they adjudge themselves to be on the polar swings of the various theoretical dimensions.

If these dichotomies were presented as one means of tidily analyzing the numerous "types" existing among individuals and nothing more, all would be well. Ever so often, however, the typologies are accompanied by value judgments which, though they may be originally avoided, creep back into the literature and/or the research as proponents of one or another type scramble for the vantage point.

The usual practice is to set up dichotomies which are superimposed over an alleged continuum and to claim value neutrality. The researchers, if not the theorists, however, proceed to treat the dichotomies not as artificial though convenient descriptions associated with an actual continuum, but as real disconnected alternatives with weightings denoting inferiority or superiority. Inappropriate research paradigms limited to the dichotomous arrangement of data are then utilized and serve ultimately only to confirm an originally false hypothesis.

Perhaps the best illustration of this flawed methodology may be taken from the literature on field-dependent versus field-independent cognitive styles. Cognitive styles have been defined as characteristic modes of functioning that we show throughout our perceptual, intellectual and social activities in a highly consistent and pervasive way. Witkin presents the dichotomy not as polar opposites of a single personality variable but as contrastive syndromes summarizing multiple variables of which the most important is an analytic ability. Further, he makes it clear that at any level of the continuum for psychological differentiation (the extent to which there is articulation within the self and between the self and the psychological field), of which field-dependence/independence are polar expressions, there are a variety of modes of integration to be found. Put simply, this means that two persons who are equally field-dependent, for example, could show vast differences in their personalities as a whole. The differences could be so great that one could be well adjusted while the other is mentally ill.

The syndrome attached to the label field-dependent is one based largely on this person's tendency to perceive stimuli globally and adhere to the organization of the prevailing field. Witkin alleged that this low tendency for perceptual analysis could be correlated with at least five broad areas of personality: controls and defenses, body concept, identity, interpersonal behaviour and cognitive restructuring skills. His research has yielded a general consistency within the following configuration of variables: poor impulse control, lack of self-esteem, undifferentiated body image, gregariousness, dependence on social cues, use of primitive defense mechanisms and poor cognitive restructuring skills.

The syndrome associated with the label field-independence assumes the presence of an ability to perceive analytically and to separate a given item from its field. The configuration of variables which has been correlated with this ability includes good impulse control, relatively high self-esteem, more differentiated, mature body image, an impersonal social orientation, non-attention to social cues unless they are task-oriented, use of more sophisticated defense mechanisms and good cognitive restructuring skills.

Witkin himself has argued that what is desirable is neither extreme field-dependence nor field-independence but the potential for flexibility on the continuum depending on the needs of the situation. Research which does not recognize this is futile.

While the theory behind field-dependence/independence in its more elaborate form appears quite commendable, the research which has ensued as well as that from which the theory was generated, has been less so. One of the greatest faults has been the growing tendency to attach value judgments to the types identified and the labels provided. To complicate matters, these judgments have been quite fickle. Thus, although the popular view in the late seventies and early eighties was that field-independent persons were more "with it" and were more "intelligent," in the late eighties and early nineties an about-turn has been witnessed. Among theorists, researchers and professionals alike, the field-dependent person is now considered by some to be more "mature" and to have the "healthier" personality. This latter view may be in keeping with the current emphasis on "sociability" in the general psychological literature. A third and more recent opinion is that the median of the continuum is most acceptable. This is partly based on Witkin's call for situational flexibility, but it is also based on the even more flimsy and superficial rationale that, statistically, the highest frequency for any personality variable in a large group will be found at the median. This third view belies the truth that there is no necessary virtue in numbers.

The Christian view refutes any notion that a given disposition is laudable on the basis of its popularity *per se*. Neither the popular, the "normal," the conventional nor even the cultural preference can be standard. Further, neither field-dependence nor field-independence nor the extremes of any other psychological variable has any intrinsic claim to holiness. There is no necessary correlation. Although the field-dependent person is more attuned to social cues, this is likely to be for selfish reasons of survival in a confused cognitive world. In addition, he may be prone towards poor control of impulses among other factors.

The field-independent person in turn, though more capable of controlling his impulses, tends to have an impersonal orientation to the world and often to be lacking in the warmth of compassion. There is therefore no indication, either theoretical or empirical, that there is any relationship at all between the character of the regenerate person and the concept field-dependence/ independence.

The same conclusion may be arrived at with respect to Rotter's internal/external "locus of control." In this theory, the issue is the degree to which the individual perceives reinforcements to be contingent on his own behaviour or with his personal characteristics. Theoretically, this psychological construct is not synonymous with self-control although it is often mistakenly held to be so. What it does do is to discuss those individuals who take full responsibility for the effects of their actions as against those who assign these effects to fate or to chance or to some external agent. An individual who demonstrates godly temperance, therefore, and who is quite capable of controlling himself, may nonetheless realize only too well that a particular group is so prejudiced that no matter what he does, his behaviour will never be properly reinforced. In this event, he is likely to be described, by definition, as having an external locus of control. At the same time, this same individual, in more propitious circumstances may be almost convinced that the world is a fair and equitable place and that he is able to predict outcomes on the basis of his actions. This being the case, he would present the profile of a person with an internal locus of control. The careful analyst understands, however, that whichever the case, this individual has internal self referents and is therefore capable of taking responsibility for his actions.

The pathetic reality is that, in psychology, these and similar dimensions, or worse, the extreme ends of such dimensions are used as the scalogram for healthy development.

If dichotomous variables such as internal versus external locus of control or moral autonomy versus heteronomy are really subjected to careful examination, it becomes apparent that some combination of the dichotomies they propose is really necessary for successful living. In addition, though each theorist would no doubt be anxious to establish his particular dimension as a governing or superordinate principle in the personality, it is clear that the dimensions are often redundant, that they even more frequently overlap, and that each and all are severely limited in their ability to describe the total person.

The call for divine control, on the other hand, is not at the outset a call for extremes, but for temperance. Once this has been established, it is necessary to understand what temperance might involve. It will at times mean moderation, but more often it may involve total abstinence or total commitment. At no time should it be regarded as moderate indulgence of the baser cravings or the *carte blanche* for mixing fleshly pleasure with devotion.

15. HUMAN "MORALITY" VERSUS DIVINE LOVE

Morality by any standard other than the Divine is feeble, unable to support itself.

For eons of time milk has been regarded as the perfect food, the "poem of plenty." It was good for the infant, the robust, the aged, the sick and the dying. When Mahatma Gandhi first arrived, upon invitation, at Buckingham Palace, it was disclosed by a bright journalist that he was received accompanied by his goat to ensure his daily supply of milk. On October 1, 1992, after so many years of promotion, health authorities in North America announced that milk, whether bovine or hircine, is not designed for human consumption!

At a higher level of thought—moral thought—human wisdom is still quite relative and is often equally fickle. The first and greatest reason for this is that man has chosen to ignore the absolute origin of all truth. He has substituted instead a multiplicity of individual perceptions, small situational truths and personally convenient doctrines. As attractive as the variety may seem, he forgets that logically and even philosophically there can be no half truths or small "t's" unless, somewhere, there is an Absolute T from which they have been derived.

The second most potent reason for the variability in man's moral thought is that he has "hitched his wagon to a star." In many instances the standard becomes the values held out by a notorious hero (whether it be the flaunted lifestyle of a movie star, a sports hero, or a party leader) or the values imposed by the bold, reckless and often ugly assertions of activist groups. These groups are often unscrupulous. Bound by the destructive results of their own choices and actions, they devote themselves with a fanatic zeal to spreading the virus. The gullible and the excitable experience no difficulty, therefore, in finding a "cause." The total result is that attitudes and lifestyles which are spurned and outlawed in one decade are unashamedly embraced and defended in the next. To a large extent, propelled by this kind of sick, spineless mentality, many are still living in the age of hedonism. Almost anything is right and can be justified. One has only to call on the half-truths of science, the still shaky though well-meaning propositions of medical knowledge and sometimes even the facade of religious cults to excuse oneself. The most popular excuse today seems to be that transgressors are not sinners but sick or genetically peculiar persons. Thus the corruption spreads and we find that "in all matters relating to the senses, mankind is experiencing an addiction of unprecedented epidemic proportions."

The overall situation regarding standards of morality today is marked by a striking contrast between human fabrication and divine investment. On the one hand, morality is totally human and societal. On the other hand, it is motivated by divine love and revelation. Since the morality usually defended by psychology as a science has tended to belong to the first category and to hold the latter in derision, it is important to examine more closely the nature of both positions. In doing so, it will be necessary to remember that morality may be distinguished from the broader subject of institutional or professional ethics on the basis of its involving personalized and intimate (often religious) decisions. It is also incumbent on the thinker involved with this subject to recall that morality has many aspects, among them 1) the rational reason for behaviour, 2) the actual transference of the decision into behaviour, 3) the ability to assess right as distinct from wrong, 4) the affective component of love, duty or loyalty as well as 5) the content of behaviour which relates to values (cultural or otherwise). In addition to these several distinct components of morality, the factor of 6) will, perseverance or endurance cannot be omitted.

HUMAN MORALITY

Human, humanistic (in its broadest sense) or natural morality, overtly and unmistakably supported by psychology, has many characteristics which go unnoticed. Like the philosophical and psychological positions from which it springs, this morality endeavours single-mindedly to promote man. It sees man as fully responsible for himself, as needing to determine and fulfill his own goals and as having only his own resources on which to rely. This is a morality which tends to shed tradition and to boast individuality and independence. Couched in the Rogerian conviction that man is basically good and that he knows what is good for him, it endeavours to take its cue from internal processes, desires and needs and to depend on the individual, existential "truth."

Quite unwittingly, and in spite of humanistic and existentialist protests to the contrary, these motives translate inevitably into a morality of self-interest and expediency. When man decides his origins and his ends, the notion of self-preservation soon invades his thinking. When there is no higher end in which he may be fulfilled, no higher power to which he must answer, all his energies and resources are geared toward his own improvement and self-actualization. Even though he may define abstract, philosophical or altruistic intentions, these easily degenerate into behaviours that are coloured by his faulty perceptions, his prejudices, his limited knowledge and, last but not least, his irrepressible ego. Perhaps one of the best examples found in psychology exists not in the content of this science *per se*, but in its methodology. In recent years we have seen the birth and growth of the Qualitative Method in research as distinct from the Quantitative Method. This method is basically anthropological in orientation and relies on the detailed observation of the subject(s) by the researcher using all manner of data-collection instruments and sources. It is presumably a disciplined attempt to extract "truth" on the basis of observed behaviour plus inference, deduction and sometimes collaborative interpretation. When properly used and applied, it has a huge potential to complement traditional quantitative research. When in the hands of the wrong person, however, the person imbued with self-interest and a driving need to succeed, what should become an honest, scientific appraisal often deteriorates into a prejudiced, hurtful violation of human rights. First, this form of research more than any other is vulnerable to the individual feelings, likes, dislikes and exaggerations of the researcher. The veracity of the report is immediately lost should the researcher become hostile to the subject. Second, in the event that the entire procedure is attempted without the subject having been consulted, the total outcome for the subject may be devastating. The intelligent subject would in no time sense what is taking place. Should he, in addition, understand the form of the method, his continuous offense at being treated as an object may become cumulative and acute. Third, at this point the well-known phenomenon of the "researcher effect" may enter the picture and the subject begins to behave unnaturally, thereby aggravating the distortions already created. The unquestionable immorality of this kind of situation, which happens all too frequently, is merely hinted at by the pathos of the following statement from ancient Greek philosophy: "Though boys throw stones at frogs in sport, the frogs do not die in sport but in sober earnest" (Bion, quoted in Plutarch: *Moralia*).

Given as it is entirely to individual knowledge and judgment and based on competition, human morality is permeated through and through with relativity. This competitive spirit of "each man for himself" is certainly as old as the human race but was no doubt heavily fuelled by the Greek humanistic ethic of aspiration, excellence or virtue of which the highest virtue was reason. Each man strove to be the best that he could in thought and reason and, consequently, man's rational or moral faculties acquired amazing capacities for making twists and turns and self-defenses.

It is not surprising that, since the age of Plato and Aristotle when Greek culture was at its height, the world has always had ready spokesmen for the rational and the relative.

Immanuel Kant's "Categorical Imperative," though claiming to be absolute in its essence, is, when properly examined, a totally relativistic route to moral judgment. "Act only" it says, "on that maxim through which you can at the same time will that it should become a universal Law" (*Metaphysics of Morals*). Though the Imperative speaks of the universal, this is a universal chosen only on the basis of individual understanding and perception. Lest this appear cynical, we should be mindful of the fact, taken from psychology itself, that human perception is at best "varyingly veridical," that is , based on, as well as containing, a modicum of error. Later, in the twentieth century, Kohlberg, inspired by Aristotle and Kant among others, presents a model for stages of development in moral thought. The sixth and highest of these stages is once again characterized by "universal ethical principles" defined as metarules for the creation of specific rules rather than as first-order rules. Among these principles are justice, the right to life, the right to property, respect for authority, society or persons, prudence, the welfare of others. Justice is regarded as the overarching and all-inclusive principle. Once again, however, when the so-called absolutes are fully explained, we understand that here too they are dependent on finite, relative human wisdom for their application. Justice, as we see in the courts of our land, is no more absolute than the wisdom of the judge by whom it is administered.

This leads to the notion that human morality is, if anything, absolutely pretentious. Can finite man really attain the dizzying heights of justice? Can man, left to his own devices, really love enough to be just? Does he know enough to be just? Does man, using his natural morality, ever achieve the wisdom of Solomon? How valid is the claim, made not only by Kohlberg but by any confirmed humanist, that human beings are sufficiently able to enter into the experience of another to be able to apprehend their pain, their needs and all the contingencies of their past or present behaviour? Does not this inexhaustible fund of knowledge require more than any one person can possess? What right has anyone, either as a self-named absolutist or relativist, to take upon himself the role of legislator or adjudicator? If morality is absolute and the standard is known to all, the individual is still bereft of total knowledge of all the circumstances. If however, morality is deemed to be relative, the predicament is even worse because neither the standard nor the circumstances are fully known. And yet this is the weighty presumption that each man takes upon himself who says that morality itself is relativistic. Is this perhaps why we have been told, *"Judge not, that ye be not judged"* (Matthew 7:1)?

As if the list of disqualifiers was not long enough, we find on inspection that human morality is riddled with conventionality. This tendency is quite strong in the twenty-first-century culture of the Western hemisphere. Ironically, while we aspire towards autonomy and disclaim the conventional, we are perhaps more conventional than we have ever been before in our history. In many walks of life and irrespective of age, there is a pressing demand today for individuality, "one-upmanship" and creativity. This is seen, for example, in the trends found among the young for leaving home, for disbanding with traditional values and parental ambitions. It is also seen in the wave of new ideologies which engulf our Western society and which vie successfully for loyalties. What is not often recognized is that these apparent pathways to "being different" often dislodge their proponents from one form of heteronomy only to thrust them into the norms of a new and sometimes less glorious group. The unwarranted substitution goes unnoticed because the change is coloured by the fad and the fashion and claims to be a part of the variety which adds spice to life. It was this breed of conventionalism, of unthinking "following the leader" which Plato dubbed as "vulgar virtue." Richard Taylor, in describing the ethic of the Modern Age as the "ethic of conventionalism," is himself quite bold in adducing causes. He claims:

> The Modern Age, more or less repudiating the idea of a divine Lawgiver, has nevertheless tried to retain the ideas of moral right and wrong, not noticing that, in casting God aside, they have also abolished the conditions of meaningfulness for moral right and wrong as well (*Ethics, Faith and Reason*).

Twenty-first-century man, no longer having a stable standard to guide his actions, sells his true God-given spontaneity for the pseudo-morality and excitement of custom, be it old or new, only to find that it has no substance.

Perhaps of all the "isms"—relativism, situationalism, conventionalism among others—it is conventionalism which is most comforting. It seems, to the natural mind, to offer the greatest security. Somewhere in the further reaches of human nature there is the recognition that there must be a standard, that morality requires something unchanging. But, unwilling to undergo the rigor of divine discipline, man decides to etch his own script and to seek company in the "normal," the indulgent and the ordinary. Situationalism, of course, takes a more extreme position. The assumption here is that the standard is always evolving so man has the right to choose his own personal code of behaviour based entirely on the nature of the situation. On the other side of the fence there are the zealots imbued with legalism of all kinds. These are they who forget that "the quality of mercy is not strained." Unfortunately, included among them are the religious legalists who turn the conscience away from duty to God towards a fanatic pharisaism.

By whatever standard, human morality in some respects is dubious or, to be more accurate, corrupt. Spinoza recognized long ago that [all too often] man uses his reason to justify what he desires:

> We neither strive for, wish, seek nor desire anything because we judge that it is good, but on the contrary, we judge something to be good because we strive for it, wish it, seek it and desire it (*Ethics*).

The Scriptures concur here, and speak of the lusts of the flesh and of the mind (Ephesians 2:3).

Psychologists today, tacitly or explicitly, customarily adopt the anthropological view that the society has the right to define virtue. Consequently, virtues become variable, subject to change and dependent on the culture or the shifting preferences and degeneracies of man. Were this the only outcome the situation would be bad enough. However, there are other consequences. If virtues, described as relatives, are variable, then vices, also conceptualized as relatives, are equally subject to changing definitions. What will happen to the human race when definitions of love and hate cross borders—when "love" becomes "hate" and "hate" becomes "love"? Perhaps this has already happened. The world once killed those whom it hated. Now it kills the unborn, the infirm and the aged in the name of love.

Rollo May, the most celebrated psychotherapist of twentieth-century America, declares that the "daimonic" (defined as benign urges for sex, passion, eros, procreation or illicit urges for hostility, rage, cruelty, the quest for power):

> must be accepted and integrated into our consciousness for psychological health to be achieved. It is all too

tempting to deal only with our virtues and repress the dark side of our personality. Such a denial of the daimonic produces a naïve innocence that often has disastrous consequences (In Kirschenbaum and Henderson, *Carl Rogers, Dialogues*).

Is it recognition and integration of the daimonic that is needed? Or do we need recognition and expulsion? *"Doth a fountain send forth at the same place sweet water and bitter?"* (James 3:11).

16. Divine Love

> He knows our need,
> To our weakness is no stranger.

THE *AGAPE*, THE GRACE OF GOD, is a tremendous subject. No one is fully competent to discuss it. And so, referring to the greatest expression of God's love, we cite the Scriptures as the purest and most authoritative source: "*God commendeth his love toward us, in that, while we were yet sinners, Christ died for us*" (Romans 5:8). This puts us on the receiving end. But the full extent of this role has not always been readily understood.

The first aspect of the *agape* is not to be found in man's charitable extensions to men, but in God's outreach to man.

The Greek term has, as its first meaning, that highest and noblest form of love which sees something infinitely precious in its object even when this object is wretched. When used in the context of Christianity, *agape* refers to the outpouring of God's love in the form of His presence, the gift of His holy Son, His favour, His blessing. It is God saying to His frail, humble and undeserving child, even before he repents, "I love you, and I have prepared a place of refuge for you. Have faith in the death of my Son for you and you shall have salvation and healing and deliverance." God's love cannot be measured. No one will ever know the depth of Christ's suffering as He bore our sin. Today, the Father is still extending this offer and showing His tender love in ways that are beyond comprehension.

The second aspect of the *agape* is the love feast. Though man's response to God is involved, it is not to be regarded as the work of man's hands but of the Spirit. The fine attunement and the fellowship are the result of the promise:

> *Behold I stand at the door and knock; if any man hear my voice, and open the door, I will come into him, and will sup with him, and he with me* (Revelation 3:20).

In this oneness of the Spirit, it is made clear that we are not to be merely recipients. The Greek origin of the word grace (*charis*) denotes not only blessing and favour, but also thankfulness. Our delight is in the Lord as He rejoices over us (see Zephaniah 3:17), so He delights in our praise:

> *Whoso offereth praise glorifieth Me, and to him that ordereth his conversation aright will I show the salvation of God* (Psalm 50:23).

The "language" of the love feast is the beauty of His presence.

Correctly understood, the love feast is not seen merely as a complement to the law; it is itself the highest and purest form of morality. The believer keeps himself in the love of God (Jude, verse 21), presenting himself, wholly, as a living sacrifice and a dwelling place unto God.

The third aspect of the *agape* is translated by Goodrich and Kohlenberger[34] as the word "it." This tiny word ("ὁ" in Greek) is defined in terms of every conceivable personal pronoun and adjective and bears the universal force of "whomsoever." It appears that it indicates, once more, the first aspect of the *agape*, God's unconditional love. But it is also reminiscent of the Great Commission: If ye love me, *"feed my sheep"* (John 21"16,17).

Divine love is not sentimentalism. Its character is a unique blend of absolute love and absolute justice: *"...whom the Lord loveth he chasteneth, and scourgeth every son whom he receiveth"* (Hebrews 12:6). It is due to this that man, made in the image of God and redeemed by Him, has the promise of reaching beyond the pseudo-universals of Kohlberg's sixth stage of moral development (justice) to a level where absolute love tempers and teaches absolute justice: *"For I desired mercy, and not sacrifice..."* (Hosea 6:6). In sharp contrast to the various ethics which have characterized the different cultures of the world, the Christian ethic is the only one which has presented the inerrant accuracy of justice in combination with the unconditional warmth of love. This is found in God alone and in His acts towards men.

There are those who believe that God's love, although absolute, is relative. Tillich says:

> The law of love is the ultimate law because it is the negation of law... The paradox of final revelation, overcoming the conflict between absolutism and relativism, is love... (Paul Tillich, *Systematic Theology*).

In saying this, allusion is made to the character of true love. Tillich then describes the ministry of Christ who went about treating each situation in a unique way and demonstrating that "love is always dependent on that which is loved." It was the concrete situation to which Jesus attended, without in any way demeaning its own peculiar character. The present author agrees that this was relativism *par excellence*. But it was more than this. It was the wisdom of God which, in itself, is also absolute.

It is at this point that more of the aberrations in psychological theories of moral development emerge clearly. One of the mainstays of Kohlberg's empirical model is the fictional "moral dilemma" of the man Heinz, with which thousands of adolescents and children were confronted during research. Heinz, a poor man whose wife is sick and dying, steals a drug from the village druggist in order to save his wife. The druggist, who had invented the medicine, had attempted to charge twice as much for it as it should have cost. At Heinz' request the druggist refused to reduce the price. Kohlberg suggests that a Stage 6 solution to the dilemma would have included the option of stealing the drug provided it was done on the basis of the universal principle of the right to life. There is, however, a caution to be observed. At no time in His ministry did Jesus ever disobey the law of God in order to fulfill either justice or love. Though His wisdom responded always to the immediate situation, He came not to destroy the law but to fulfill it (Matthew 5:17). In God's absolute economy, stealing is always an offense. Do those who support the Kohlbergian view consider the option of trust in a wise, loving and all-knowing God?

Divine love is exquisitely depicted by the metaphor of human marriage. In the Old Testament, Israel, the chosen people of the Father, are called to be His bride. In the book of

THE GROWTH OF THE PERSON

Hosea, God weeps over His bride declaring that though she has chosen other gods, He will love her with an everlasting love. In the New Testament, the Church, the Lamb's bride, waits for the day of the great marriage feast. Nothing can separate the Lord's bride from Him but sin. Sin is described with vigorously graphic language as the "whoredom" of Israel. But with ever-renewed love and forgiveness the people are called to repentance.

Essentially, the believer is called to live the life of love:

> *Love suffers long and is kind; love does not envy; love does not parade itself; is not puffed up; does not behave rudely, does not seek its own, is not provoked, thinks no evil; does not rejoice in iniquity, but rejoices in the truth; bears all things, believes all things, hopes all things, endures all things... And now abide faith, hope, love, these three; but the greatest of these is love* (1 Corinthians 13:4-7,13 NKJV).

Understanding the *agape* fully requires us to go back in time to the earlier culture of the Hebrews and to the word *henl* which meant, "to bend, to stoop." God condescends to stoop and touch us with His favour, though there is nothing in us that deserves being noticed or touched or blessed. We are of infinite worth to Him without being worthy.

> Love that goes upward is worship; love that goes outward is affection; love that stoops is grace (Donald Grey Barnhouse, *Romance; Man's Ruin*).

17. DISCIPLINE

ONE OF THE MOST ANCIENT CONCEPTIONS of discipline, the one which comes readily to mind whether we proceed to embrace it or reject it, is the Old Testament warning, *"He that spareth his rod hateth his son; but he that loveth him chasteneth him betimes"* (Proverbs 13:24).

What is the rod? Almost to a man, the psychologists of today would shake their heads in dismay at this Old Testament injunction. This is not to say that the psychological understanding of discipline is superior. Without exception, every psychological school of thought on the subject of discipline wrests it from its true essence in order to keep it firmly planted on the level of the terrestrial. Among the behaviourists (see, for example, Skinner), the concept of discipline reinvokes the notion of unfailing reinforcement or reward for good behaviour. The debate regarding what to do with bad behaviour still rages, most apparently inclined to think that persistent application of reinforcers for good behaviour will eventually erode the incidence of the bad. Among the humanists, too, there is an abhorrence for punishment and a simultaneous affectation of respect for and indulgence towards the naughty child. There is a conviction that the child should be "made to know the limits," yet, at the same time, we are instructed that the child himself "knows what is good for him" (see, for example, Rogers). In this respect few humanists, such as Maslow and Erikson, stand head and shoulders above Rogers and his peers. Although Maslow agrees with Rogers that our innate "instinctoid" needs for security, love, self-actualization, among others, are predominantly healthy and benign, both Maslow and Erikson are quick to understand that these "instinct-remnants" are only very weak fragments, easily overwhelmed by the far more powerful forces of learning and culture.

> The human needs... are weak and feeble rather than unequivocal and unmistakable; they whisper rather than shout. And the whisper is easily drowned out (Maslow, *Motivation and Personality*).

Speaking more directly on the subject of discipline Maslow adds:

> All we have are strong suspicions, widespread clinical impressions, the slowly hardening opinion of child psychologists and educators that merely and only basic need gratification is not enough, but that some experience with firmness, toughness, frustration, discipline and limits is also needed by the child... basic need gratification so eas-

ily slips over into unbridled indulgence, self-abnegation, total permissiveness, over protection, toadyism. Love and respect for the child must at the very best be integrated with love and respect for oneself as a parent and for adulthood in general. Children are certainly persons but they are not experienced persons... (*Motivation and Personality*).

Among the cognitivists (Baumrind, for example) there is an admirable attempt to combine parental warmth with the induction of the rational and the realistic. The child must be helped to understand why an action is wrong and be able to appreciate the inevitable consequences.

While each of the preceding attitudes may or may not have a valid contribution to make, none has succeeded in grasping the central truth of discipline. Although arresting, it is often overlooked that the root meaning of the word discipline is "disciple." Etymologically, the Latin terms *discipulus* (disciple), *discere* (to teach) and *disciplina* (instruction) are all interrelated. When they are translated into the context of Christianity, without deviation or modification of any kind, discipline is understood as the faithful act of following the Master. Nor is there any doubt as to what the follower is to do. Jesus Himself, preempting the issue, declared, *"The words that I speak unto you, they are spirit and they are life"* (John 6:63). The inference, as always, is that *"to obey is better than sacrifice"* (1 Samuel 15:22).

Discipline, therefore, is all about relationship—relationship with God and relationship with man. The colour, form and dress of this relationship is the inerrant example of Christ. The breath and life of the relationship is the presence of God Himself.

In order for discipline or discipleship to filter through to the minutiae of everyday living, every aspect of human development must be touched and transformed. The content of Figure 6 explains graphically how discipleship relates to aspects of development as well as how these developmental components interrelate. For the true disciple, Christ Himself must be in command of all six aspects of the personality: spiritual, social, moral, emotional, intellectual and physical alike. It is notable that as He addresses the various dimensions of our lives, and as we yield and obey, the product of our commitment in the various domains is neither static, contained nor expended but flows back to increase the richness and fullness of our spiritual experience. In saying this, certain assumptions are made. Figure 6 expresses the conviction that it is the spiritual dimension, the experience of the indwelling God or the relationship with God through Christ, which is the dominant and integrative directive in the personality. While all dimensions interrelate, therefore, the spiritual must of necessity command the hierarchy. It is the starting point of the entire process as well as the preserving point of contact, the *sine qua non*.

It is understood that this belief, supported by Scripture, has not always been expressed even by the more stable forces in our society. The Ontario Ministry of Education Guidelines, prompted perhaps by its peculiar interpretation of the limited role of the school, forsake the commanding heights of the spiritual entirely and places religious education in the fine print of their catalogue. It also tends to assign equal importance to the remaining components. On a less formal level, the youthful voice of the student, influenced no doubt by convention, can still be heard: "Some people say that in order to be spiritual, you have to be social," or, even more pathetic, "I think that the physical dimension is the key to personality."

There is no gainsaying the fact that sin, on any of these levels including the physical, will adversely affect, if not totally destroy, our relationship with God. It is equally evident, however, that we do not come into relationship with God through the body but through the spirit. God is Spirit and He must be worshipped in the Spirit. Further, it is the spirit of man that is eternal; the body, being only temporal, perishes and dies. The spiritual dimension, therefore, can never be subordinate to the physical. Nor can it be subordinate to the social. *"Thou shalt love the Lord thy God with all thy heart..."* (Matthew 22:37) is still the first Commandment.

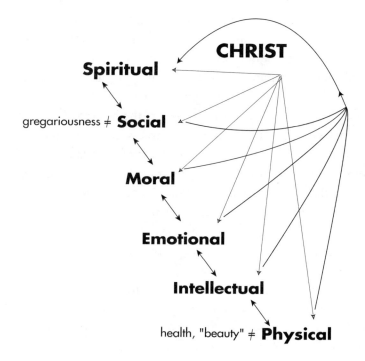

Figure 6 - ASPECTS OF DEVELOPMENT AND RELATIONSHIP IN DISCIPLESHIP

A precise indication of the nature of each of the six dimensions is in order since popular definitions appear to be the frequent cause of confusion and require clarification. The "spiritual" cannot be defined merely as relationship, since this would simply leave it on the level of the social. Spirituality, in the Christian context, is relationship with God which is evidenced by His presence and seen in our character. The man spoke true who declared, "Shrouds have no pockets. Your character is the only thing you can take to heaven with you." On the other hand, the "social" does not speak primarily to the habit of gregariousness but to the quality of human relationship. As Figure 5 discloses, the truly social person is not the one who gravitates towards crowds but the one who, regardless of how minimal the contact may be, has the sincere capacity for compassion and love, to give the "cup of cold water." The "moral" is distinguished as the human ability to recognize and deal with notions and practices related to right versus wrong. It therefore forms the basis of all relationships, both social and spiritual, but it is itself a result not primarily a cause of the spiritual. The "emotional" and "intellectual," as polar opposites, are demarcated by the rational. While the intellect expresses the noetic, the mental or the rational, the term "emotion" describes a strong surge of feeling marked by an impulse to outward expression and often accompanied by complex bodily reactions. It is noteworthy that it is derived from the Latin *e* (out) + *movere* (to move). The emotional is therefore more inclusive of the total person than the intellectual and is closer to the spirit. A word of caution is perhaps in order. The term "mind," as used in Scripture, refers to the emotions as well as behaviour and is certainly more than intellect. In the present model (Figure 6), the term "physical" refers to the material tangible body and its properties without any necessary denotation of its state of health or its degree of natural beauty. With these definitions, it is believed that the rationale for the hierarchy in Figure 6 is obvious. In Christian dogma the body is regarded as temporary, not eternal. *"Though the outward man perish, the inner man is renewed day by day"* (2 Corinthians 4:16).

Contrary to practice, this discussion on discipline will not intrude into the area of strategies for order and good government in spite of the fervency with which such strategies are entertained in so many educational and psychological settings.

True discipline, whether of the self or of those in one's charge, is not a question of the judicious use of strategies. It is the clear response to the presence and the will of God by the individual. In the case of the pedagogue, it is normally influenced both by precept and by example.

In the quest for perfection (which should be the aim of all human endeavour) we recognize good wherever this appears and do not strive to throw away or reject out of hand the possibility of making the good better and the better best. The tragedy is where excellence is professed before it is realized and the ideal is regarded as beyond the reach of grasping hands which begin to say that since the grapes could not be gathered, they must be sour. The greater tragedy is seen when we wrest this work of perfection from the hands of God and attempt to effect it on our own. The power of the commandment, *"Be ye therefore perfect, even as your Father which is in Heaven is perfect"* (Matthew 5:48) is then lost and any strategies which we may introduce become febrile and ineffective.

Excellence in discipline which is obtainable from the home-sewn, home-grown vintage, will not be achieved by the sophistications of an intellectual or social domestic culture but by the humble values of a home which recognizes that the Creator is

Head. By the same token, discipline will neither be achieved by experimental laxities nor by the iron fist of a dictator but by recognition of the only Teacher who could say "Follow Me."

The produce of victory which is home-grown and home-spun is available for export abroad to the glory of God.

18. Trust in God versus Basic Anxiety

THE PSYCHOLOGICAL THEORIES dealing with anxiety have treated the phenomenon, properly or improperly, totally on the level of the natural. The explanations provided by the various models taken from the major schools of thought—whether psychoanalysis, behaviourism or humanism—are complementary in their distinctiveness. At the same time, they all contribute with an almost obstinate connivance to the avoidance and concealment of the cardinal role of the supernatural. More specifically, the explanation of healthy personality provided in the Gospels appears to be shunned as questionable material.

Freud's psychoanalytic view of anxiety was tripartite. He believed that the ego, which normally assists the individual to mediate the problems of the environment, if weak or weakened, would be subject to "reality anxiety." On its own, the *id*, the source of libidinal instincts and uncontrolled drives, if allowed by the weak ego to get out of hand, becomes the prime source of "neurotic anxiety." Conversely, the superego or conscience, if allowed by the ego to be too overbearing, degenerates into the complexity of "moral anxiety."

The neo-Freudian, Erikson, in an attempt to minimize the checks and counter-checks of a "mechanistic" personality and to assign to the ego a role which was greater than effecting the truce between the id and the superego, presents the ego as a potentially integrative power which moves towards integrity in social context. One of its prime functions is to define the identity of the individual, a task which reaches the crisis point during adolescence. Identity must subsume the satisfactory solutions to all previous personality conflicts beginning with that of the struggle between trust versus mistrust in infancy. If this identity is not achieved in adolescence, the result is identity diffusion, an acute form of anxiety. Each successive conflict or crisis in the Eriksonian stages is embedded, in one way or another, either in the propitious or in the threatening and life-crushing nature of the social context, giving to this theory a decidedly humanistic impact.

Another neo-Freudian, Horney, explains neurotic anxiety by placing even greater emphasis on the relationship or lack thereof between the individual and the social context. To Horney, neurotic anxiety results from disturbed interpersonal relationships during childhood. This is itself the result of pathogenic parental behaviours: domination, overprotectiveness, overindulgence, humiliation, derision, brutality and perfectionism, hypocrisy, inconsistency, partiality to other siblings, blind adoration, neglect. That is:

> ...the people in the environment are too wrapped up in their own neuroses to be able to love the child, or even conceive of him as the particular individual he is... as a result, the child does not develop a feeling of belonging, of "we" but instead a profound insecurity and vague apprehensiveness for which I use the term basic anxiety (K. Horney, *Neurosis and Human Growth: The Struggle towards Self-Realization*).

In this situation the child,

> ...cannot express his feelings honestly. He cannot simply like or dislike, trust or distrust, express his wishes or protest against those of others, but has automatically to devise ways to cope with people and to manipulate them with minimum damage to himself (Horney).

All of this breeds a dismal deep-seated insecurity. The neurotic has one of three main solutions to basic anxiety. The first, helplessness (a moving toward people), involves excessive desire for protection. The second, aggression (moving against people), involves pronounced wishes for domination and mastery. The third, the detached withdrawal (a moving away from people), emphasizes isolation and marked avoidance of others.

Mowrer, who appears to have sensibly combined aspects of psychoanalysis and behaviourism, goes a step beyond the Freudian school. For Mowrer, neuroticism is not due simply to basic anxiety. Rather, it is the culminating point of a grandiose effort to *repress* chronic anxiety:

> This conscious repudiation of conscience does not mean that its forces are nullified. They are merely muted. Their signals are distorted and delayed. Instead of being experienced promptly and explicitly as conscience guilt, they appear in the form of depression, anxiety, self-

derogation. Since these states are thus dissociated from the circumstances and events that occasion them, they appear to be alien to the personality, unrealistic, irrational, abnormal (H.O. Mowrer, *Learning Theory and Personality Dynamics*).

Put more simply, the neurotic does not "do business" with his conscience, but has a tendency to distrust and repress it. Because of resistances set up by the ego and the ensuing split between the ego and the superego (the dictates of the conscience acquired primarily through interaction with primary caretakers), the ego regresses to a more infantile, id-dominated and asocial state.

It is the phenomenon of repression that creates the difference between normal fear (specific stimulus) and normal anxiety (nonspecific source) on one hand and neurotic anxiety on the other. Normal anxiety is neither 1) disproportionate to the objective threat, nor 2) associated with repression of anxiety, nor 3) requiring of neurotic defense mechanisms. Further, it is the elimination of repression which is seen as essential for the pain of neurotic anxiety to be transformed back into a normal fear.

Unlike the criminal, then, Mowrer holds that the neurotic still has a conscience strong enough to bother him, but like the criminal, his conscience tends to be disfigured, immature, irresponsible and antisocial.

The cognitive theorist, Berlyne, suggests that anxiety (very high arousal related to activity in the Reticular Activating System [RAS] of the mid-brain) is induced by an environment that is either too high or too low in arousal potential. This theory is supported by that of the neo-behaviourist, Hebb, who demonstrated that very high arousal is itself detrimental to optimal performance and will lead to increased emotional disturbance and/or disorganized behaviour. Eysenck has found that high arousal/anxiety is related to introversion as distinct from extroversion. One may justifiably wonder whether the high arousal level of introverts is due to their efforts to repress the conscience. Eysenck himself, however, suggests that introversion is at right angles with neuroticism, that is, uncorrelated, leading to the conclusion that it is equally possible for extroverts to be neurotic. This seems consistent with the real world where many examples may be found of extroverted persons who appear to be animatedly attempting to cover up a worrying conscience. "Low arousal" in the extrovert may be due, then, only to a dying or almost-dead conscience.

The humanist, Rogers, has much to say about anxiety. In the fashion of most humanists, however, it is not quite clear whether anxiety precedes and is the cause of poor self-concept or whether poor self-concept brings about anxiety, or both. What is abundantly clear is that humanists tend to accept the self-concept as the generative centre of the entire personality.

A number of models have already been set out in this present work to explain the regenerate person and his development. In this section, the view is presented with greater affirmation that healthy personality is related to but not primarily dependent either on particular types or traits or on the self-concept or on identity or even on the conscience. The model seen in Figure 7 is based on the belief that healthy personality is primarily dependent on the presence of God in the person's life and the condition of the heart before Him. This will include the status of the conscience, the quality of the self-concept and the satisfactory achievement of identity among other conditions. With this as its chief message, the model goes beyond the propositions given by Mowrer, Erikson, Horney among others by leaps and bounds.

TRUST IN GOD	BASIC ANXIETY

New Birth
Love of God
Trust, obedience, submission, dependence, cherishing (i.e. worship)
 	
Love (acceptance) of self
Self-interest NOT self-adulation
 	
Love (acceptance) of others
Cherishing, striving for their good, giving, doing, hoping, praying for their best
 	
Rest
Covered by Christ's righteousness
Seeing oneself as having unlimited worth although unworthy of God's love
 	
If there is sin;
    admission, repentance, forgiveness
 	
Prayer: supplication versus anxiety
 	
Fruit of the Spirit:
    love, joy, peace, long-suffering, gentleness, goodness, faith, meekness, temperance
	Basic anxiety, fear
	Sin
	Lack of trust in God
	
	Failure to love God
	Failure to love self
	Failure to love others
	
	Guilt, high arousal
	
	Poor self-concept (Coopersmith)
	
	If No Repentance
	Unconfessed guilt
	
	Possible extreme introversion
	Possible extreme extroversion
	  (Eysenck)
	Possible withdrawal
	Possible aggression
	Possible helplessness etc.
	  (Horney)
	Repression of Anxiety (Mowrer)
	Excessive energy used to deny, cover guilt
	Does not "do business" with conscience
	Neuroticism
	Fear of others
	
	Demonic forces easily enter to feed on fear, anxiety
	Invasion of privacy
	Greater attempt to repress conscience.
	Anxiety exacerbated
	Psychoticism
	
	Spiritual Death

Figure 7 - TRUST IN GOD VERSUS BASIC ANXIETY

Figure 7 explains the phenomenon of the absence or presence of anxiety by contrasting life subsequent to the new birth with the life of sin.

The new birth takes place at the point in the person's life when, regardless of personality traits and predispositions but by an act of volition and trust, he makes Jesus Christ his Saviour and Lord. The "beloved Son" of God grants the person His righteousness and becomes his Example, his Friend, his Healer and his King. What follows from this is revolutionary—not "of the flesh" but heavenly. The individual begins to walk "in the Spirit." The sequence indicated in the left flow chart of Figure 7 is set in action. Motivated purely by his love for God, self and other, in accordance with the will of God, the individual is able to enjoy divine Rest or peace.

Critics may be quick to assert that this model makes it appear that sin and its consequent distance from God is the sole cause of anxiety, that there are millions of people who are good, "moral" persons, not given to the practice of sin, who are nonetheless anxious. They may therefore be prone to settle for one of a million psychological reasons for the cause of anxiety. The answer to the critic, however, is that in the light of Philippians chapter 2 (*"Be anxious for nothing, but by prayer and supplication, with thanksgiving, let your requests be made known to God"*), chronic anxiety is sin. It involves disobedience and lack of trust.

The biblical explanation of basic anxiety and its complication is presented in the right column of Figure 7. The model acknowledges that basic anxiety is the root of all evil; but the basic anxiety sometimes observed in infancy is not sin. Due to the fallen condition of the human race, the innocence of the young is often harassed by pernicious and relentless anxiety in the form of personality predispositions and "hand-me-down" genes, for example, the fretful infant or the withdrawn child. If this is not corrected but facilitated by the various environments in which the child finds himself, and allowed to become chronic, it becomes sin. The failure to trust God provokes a heightened sense of guilt which, with its concomitants (see Figure 7), causes an exponential curve in anxiety. The Eriksonian hypothesis is, of course, that guilt is the converse of initiative. It is easily seen, however, that lack of initiative may itself be a result of basic or chronic anxiety. In fact, the Eriksonian concept of "mistrust," at the very beginning of his bipolar crises, suggests the possibility of a pervasive anxiety at the beginning of life; that is, all the negatives in Erikson's schedule could be said to have some relevance to early anxiety.

While the Eriksonian "crises" are compatible with the biblical presentation of basic anxiety and its aberrations, the psychological theory is not really adequate for the task of explaining the phenomenon. A crucial point in the healing of the individual is his willingness to repent and to surrender his carnal ways. The act of repentance will clear the channels for God to communicate with man. Without repentance, there will be further personality perversions. Should the individual push aside his God-given sense of responsibility and delay repentance, it is likely that he will also attempt to repress his anxiety. According to Mowrer, it is the repression of anxiety, or the refusal to "do business" with one's conscience, not anxiety *per se*, which leaves the individual prey to neuroticism. In biblical terms, this is tantamount to an acute lack of honesty with oneself and with God. This split in the conscience could pave the way for the entry of demonic forces which feed on anxiety and fear and in turn create greater havoc.

The only antidote to neuroticism and psychoticism is repentance before God, cleansing and faith in Christ. *"Perfect love casteth out fear"* (1 John 4:18). There is no fear in love.

Truth knows no fear. Jesus said, *"I am the way, the truth and the life. No man cometh to the Father but by me"* (John 14:6).

The psychological attempt to cure anxiety falls far short of adequacy in many other ways. For example, those who claim (e.g. Aaron Beck and Albert Ellis) that personality problems may be healed by "good thinking," place on the sick a burden that is often far beyond their capabilities. The human mind, *per se*, is not strong enough to withstand the invasion of the enemy and his "shenanigans." The Bible says, *"When the enemy shall come in like a flood, the Spirit of the Lord shall lift up a standard against him"* (Isaiah 59:19). This is a promise, a warranty. It is also the birthright of every believer. Peace is not a fabrication of man's mind. It is a gift from God. Personality begins in the heart of man, not in his mind.

The answer to the question of irregularities in the personality can be found in Christ by each seeker for himself. This is the glorious provision of the Gospel.

A careful analysis will therefore convince the reader that the treatment of anxiety is pursued both by the psychologist and the theologian. The difficulty rests in the fact that the psychologist deals with the subject on one level while it is clear that the subject itself cannot be reached with mere mortal tools and material implements as it has dimensions which are beyond the natural. Here is a disparity if ever there was one.

Conclusion:

Sabbatismos

> *There remaineth therefore a rest to the people of God. For he that is entered into his rest, he also hath ceased from his own works, as God did from his* (Hebrews 4:9-10).

Psychikos. Man without the Spirit. Man attempting to do everything by himself and for himself. Man relying on his mind. An amazing concept and a dangerous one!

I do not here refer to the brain. We have discovered enough about the brain to know that it is the most complicated and efficient switchboard in the world and that we have a very far way to go in order to plumb its mysteries.[35] But the brain is only a complex physical structure—an obedient servant of the mind. The neurochemical activity and electrical impulses and reactions which characterize the proper functioning of the brain are related to but not necessarily the origin and cause of mind. They may also be the result of mind. The current fad in psychology for pointing to the excess or deficiency of specific chemicals in the brain as an explanation of personality traits, aberrations and mental or physical illnesses is convenient but erroneous. There is no doubt that the body (including its brain) is subject to non-propitious circumstances such as lack of opportunity for exercise or poor nutrition. The biblical position on all ill-health, however, supports the view that, more often than not, it is the presence of spirit which adversely affects the mind and its thoughts which in turn create imbalances in both the body and its brain. Man is the product of his thoughts. Angry, spiteful, fearful or undisciplined thought produces specific noxious substances in the body.[36] To an even greater extent, man is his heart. The presence of spirit which is evil turns and corrupts both mind and heart. The only power which can successfully resist the power of evil is the Spirit of God Himself. It is due to the primacy of spirit in spiritual, psychological and physical health, that we are told *"God... breathed into man the breath of life, and man became a living soul"*(Genesis 2:7). It is for this reason that on so many occasions, Jesus healed the sick, giving the spiritual panacea, *"... sin no more, lest a worse thing come unto thee"* (John 5:14). It is for this reason that the Lord Jesus Himself, when He was to be tempted, was led up into the mountains by the Holy Spirit. He did not go there alone.

The pathetic irony of the humanistic position is that while the baser sins are regarded with due contempt, it is not realized that aspirations for and devotion to self-reliance, self-sufficiency, self-glorification, and even self-actualization all betray a basic attitude of sin and a corruption of spirit. These attitudes now tend to colour most, if not all, of psychology and its tenets.

The problems in any human life are often numerous. Little man, with his chronic myopia, is all too prone to see only the physical, social and emotional causes of dysfunction. To make the matter worse, psychology, which is the science for the betterment of man's behaviour, has stubbornly refused to remember or even acknowledge that man is also a moral and primarily a spiritual being. It appears that his most significant problems are constantly being kept out of the office and shoved into the waiting room.

To some extent, psychology takes its cue from current opinion. As a result, some aberrations of spirit, soul and body are smiled at since they have acquired social acceptability. In this category are, to varying degrees, intoxication, homosexuality, lack of fidelity. Other categories of disorders, however, which have not passed forgiven and unnoticed due to conventional public alarm are hurried into the emergency room for immediate attention. These include obesity, anorexia, drug use, battered wife syndrome and child abuse. But there is no consistent concern in all of this for the supernatural and even less for the will of God. Destructive styles of life are put in the acceptable/ non-acceptable categories purely on the basis of social whim. In many cases biblical standards have been so long ago dismissed that they are relegated as explanations for the "immature" or the "fanatic."

At a time when there is a march against legalism, when anti-legalists have suddenly become aggressive and even belligerent, there are, ironically, certain aspects of grace which need to be remembered. Christ came not to destroy but to fulfill the law. The most beautiful of the many experiences of God's grace is the prayer, "Since I cannot obey your law by myself, Lord, please help me." Redeeming grace is saving grace but it is also keeping grace. Of course, it is not the pharisaical, ritualistic law to which reference is made here; rather, it is the law of life: *"Thou shalt love the Lord thy God with all thine heart, and... thy neighbour as thyself"* (Matthew 22:37,39).

The psychological approach to unhealthy personality is "Mind, cure thyself." The Christian approach to the ills that beset man is first of all submission to the Son of Man who is "Lord of the Sabbath" (Luke 6:5). It is Jesus, *Yeshua*, who leads His people into the Promised Land. He is our Sabbath.

The appeal to enter into the Sabbath rest is made to all manner of sick as well as to the so-called "healthy." The Gospel picture of mankind is that we all have sinned and *"come short of the glory of God"* (Romans 3:23). While cognitivism, behaviourism and humanism each tries, in its own frenzied way, to explain and adjust the mechanisms that have gone wrong, and to make sense out of the million psychological variables that interact one with the other, the Lord Jesus simply says—*"Come unto me, all ye that labour and are heavy laden, and I will give you rest!"* (Matthew 11:28).

The recovery of the unhealthy and the development of the healthy are pressing problems which, alike, require more than the illumination of man's mind. Psychology's major problem is that while it is calling for "good thinking" as a remedy for man's ills, it is forced to admit that the mind itself is easily subject to the vagaries of heredity, as well as of the physical and social environment, and it is easily led astray by its own infirmities and misperceptions. In twentieth-century psychology, the best-kept secret has been the fact that what man needs for optimal development is the illuminating Light of the Spirit of God. Having left out the Spirit of God, psychology is ill-equipped either to give a proper exposition of the nature of man's personality or to indicate the remedy for his ills and the proper course of his development. This work does not profess to have shown all the disparities existing between psychology and Christianity but has selected some of the major cases.

The issue, therefore, is Jesus. And the question is, "What will psychology do with Jesus who is called the Christ?" Is psychology going to accept this Jesus as the sin offering and the propitiation with authority to say, "go and shut down the practice of sin" so that the creatures can enter into the rest which remains to the people of God?

Holiness is entirely an attribute of God, whether we are speaking of it obliquely in reference to things or to titles or to human beings. Once it is approached characteriologically, it is God's—and God's alone. This attribute stands out as the first quality in Yahweh, embracing all His other qualities:

> As the sun's rays, combining all the colours of the spectrum, come together in the sun's shining and blend into light, so in His self-manifestation all the attributes of God come together and blend into holiness (J.D. Douglas, *The New Bible Dictionary*).

Nor should God's being and character be conceived of as merely a synthesis of abstract perfections. This would be to deprive God of all reality. God is Spirit and the work of His Spirit in the life of a man is His gift to man:

> *If ye then, being evil, know how to give good gifts unto your children, how much more shall your heavenly Father give the Holy Spirit to them that ask him?* (Luke 11:13).

The one conclusion that every argument and chapter in this work leads to may be put in simple but profound terms. If we desire to be holy *"for the temple of God is holy, which temple [we] are"* (1 Corinthians 3:17), if we seek growth and success in terms of the fulfillment of our God-given destiny, we must become as lambs. This may require the ability to be silent at times—*"He was oppressed, and he was afflicted, yet he opened not his mouth"* (Isaiah 53:7)—but it will certainly mean a responsiveness to God's love, a docility, a desire to be shorn of self, a willingness to be led, and, perhaps, even to be carried.

Endnotes

[1] See Carl Rogers' description of his early life including the changes in his religious convictions—C.R. Rogers, *On Becoming a Person: A Therapist's View of Psychotherapy*, and C.R. Rogers, *Autobiography*. In E.G. Boring and G. Lindzey (Eds) *A History of Psychology in Autobiography*. Rogers' claim, that the most fundamental level of the human being is essentially good, benign and positive, would seem to be in conflict with the Prophets who said, *The heart is deceitful above all things, and desperately wicked* (Jeremiah 17:9).

[2] C.G. Jung, *Memories, Dreams, Reflections*.

[3] The concept of self-actualization is explained at length in later sections of this work. Its most outstanding proponents in the recent literature are Abraham Maslow and Carl Rogers.

[4] H.L. Ansbacher, Alfred Adler and G. Stanley Hall, "Correspondence and General Relationship;" *Journal of the History of the Behavioural Sciences*.

[5] A. Bandura, "The Self System in Reciprocal Determinism;" *American Psychologist*.

[6] Jean-Jacques Rousseau, *Emile*.

[7] Carl Rogers, *On Becoming a Person*.

[8] Abraham Maslow, *Motivation and Personality*.

[9] For example, Professor Barry Beyerstein of Simon Fraser University. This was disclosed during a televised interview on "Petrie in Prime," 3 August, 1993. Beyerstein claims that the brain alone can explain all "outer body" experiences.

[10] See Kirschenbaum and Henderson (Eds) *Carl Rogers: Dialogues*.

[11] The confusion created by the Greek "sarx" is apparent rather than real since the New Testament itself clarifies the problem.

[12] Glen Whitlock, "The Structure of Personality in Hebrew Psychology. In H. Newton Malony (ed.), *Wholeness and Holiness: Readings in the Psychology/Theology of Mental Health*.

[13] Ruth Beechick, *A Biblical Psychology of Learning: How Your Mind Works*.

[14] J.R. Fleck and J.D. Carter (Eds) *Psychology and Christianity: Integrative Readings*.

[15] A discussion on "Problems in the Measurement of Religion" is found in Kenneth E. Hyde, *Religion in Childhood and Adolescence*.

[16] A significant proposition within the Piagetian theory is that children, at approximately age 6, 7, acquire the logical skills to carry out "conservation" tasks. A child is able to conserve

if he recognizes that a change in one property of an object, (be it number, length, shape, distribution, etc.) does not automatically effect changes in other properties of the object.

17 "Animistic thinking" is explained by Piaget as the tendency children have to attribute life to any or all moving objects, for example, the sun, stars, the waves of the sea, a kite.

18 Allport's term "intrinsic" religion describes the person whose faith depends on internal frames of reference. This person is committed to Relationship with God. "Extrinsic" religion is akin to "religiosity," demonstrates a utilitarian approach to religion and is more often than not legalistic. The frames of reference are relatively externalized. See Gordon Allport and J.M. Ross, "Personal Religious Orientation and Prejudice," *Journal of Personality and Social Psychology*.

19 This author believes that the inclusion of Mary's case history in Fowler's Stages of Faith was an unfortunate and confusing selection. Since Mary's "initial" conversion appears to have affected only her ego, the greater part of her story is not illustrative of Redeeming Grace, nor can it easily be located in Fowler's cognitive stages for the same reason. Fowler himself experiences difficulty in categorizing her and eventually places her in both stages 3 and 5. See also Kenneth Hyde's *Religion in Childhood and Adolescence*.

20 K. Hyde, *Religion in Childhood and Adolescence*.

21 MacMain, J.S., "An Empirical Study of the Reasons for Young Adult Participation or Nonparticipation Within Local Churches," 1980. Quoted in K. Hyde.

22 Marcia, J.E., "Development and Validation of Ego-Identity Status," *Journal of Personality and Social Psychology*.

23 See, for example, Robert Kail, *The Development of Memory in Children*.

24 Richard Taylor, *Ethics, Faith and Reason*.

25 E.J. Mischey, "Faith, Identity and Morality in Late Adolescence," *Character Potential*.

26 For example, see Martin and Deidre Bobgan, *The Psychological Way/ The Spiritual Way*.

27 See Theodore Mischel (Ed), *The Self: Psychological and Philosophical Issues*.

28 J.D. Douglas, *The New Bible Dictionary*.

29 For example, Adorno, *The Authoritarian Personality*.

30 J.E. Dittes, "Justification by Faith and the Experimental Psychologist," *Religion in Life*. Quoted in James Michael Lee (Ed.), *Handbook of Faith*.

31 Ralph W. Hood and Ronald J. Morris, "Conceptualization of Quest: A Critical Rejoinder to Batson," *Review of Religious Research*.

32 Quoted in Hyde, *Religion in Childhood and Adolescence*.

33 See for example, Rogers, C.R., "A Theory of Therapy, Personality, and Interpersonal Relationships, as developed in the Client-Centered Framework." In Koch (Ed.), *Psychology: A Study of a Science*.

34 Goodrick and Kohlenberger, *The NIV Exhaustive Concordance*.

35 Richard Restak, *The Brain*.

36 Ibid.